MW01075742

PRAISE FOR
THE BASICS IN 21 DAYS

"Benjamin Williams has written a key book to help any believer get started in a spirit-filled journey. I highly recommend this book as a foundation-laying guide to a meaningful and powerful walk with God."

–Randy Clark, president and founder, Global Awakening Ministries

"*The Basics in 21 Days* is an awesome way to begin your journey with God. Each short, easy-to-read chapter will take you one step further in faith. Every new Christian should read it carefully and then read it again!"

–J. Lee Grady, contributing editor, *Charisma Magazine*

"I was raised in a church, but I never really got anything out of it, and kind of just lived my life how I felt I should live it. Then, God got a hold of my heart and started to show me new things. I wasn't sure what to do with the stuff I was learning, but this book (*The Basics in 21 Days*) really explained a lot and helped me day by day to learn things in a more basic way. The Scripture references really helped me get into my Bible."

—Rose, New Believer

"I love the Basics in 21 days! It helped me to find my secret place with Jesus and I hear him much more clearly now! The questions in the book led me to ask more questions & listen for answers. Then I realized I was just having conversations with Jesus all the time! This book is so well written and very easy to follow! I encourage Christians of all ages to read this book! You will cherish the time you spend with Jesus & long for more!"

—Heather

**THE BASICS
IN 21 DAYS**

Benjamin & Micah Joy Williams

**THE BASICS
IN 21 DAYS**

The Basics In 21 Days
Copyright © 2011 by Benjamin & Micah Joy Williams. All rights reserved.

No part of this publication may be reproduced, stored in a retrieval system or transmitted in any way by any means, electronic, mechanical, photocopy, recording or otherwise without the prior permission of the author except as provided by USA copyright law.

All scripture quotations, unless otherwise indicated, are taken from the *New American Standard Bible* ©, Copyright © 1960, 1962, 1963, 1968, 1971, 1972, 1973, 1975, 1977, 1995 by The Lockman Foundation. Used by permission.

Scripture quotations marked (KJV) are taken from the *Holy Bible, King James Version*, Cambridge, 1769. Used by permission. All rights reserved.

Scripture quotations marked (NIV) are taken from the *Holy Bible, New International Version* ©, NIV ©. Copyright © 1973, 1978, 1984 by Biblica, Inc.??Used by permission of Zondervan. All rights reserved worldwide. www.zondervan.com

Scripture quotations marked (NKJV) are taken from the *New King James Version* ©. Copyright © 1982 by Thomas Nelson, Inc. Used by permission. All rights reserved.

The opinions expressed by the author are not necessarily those of Tate Publishing, LLC.

Original cover and interior design by Emily Mabry, sparrowinkdesign.com.
Updates by Lance Waldrop, Chelsea Womble, and Joseph Cotten.

Published in the United States of America

1. Religion, Christian Life, Inspirational
2. Religion, Christian Theology, General
11.08.02

TABLE OF CONTENTS

INTRODUCTION 9

DAY 1: VOICE OF GOD..12

DAY 2: THE KINGDOM...21

DAY 3: BELONGING..26

DAY 4: THE BIBLE...31

DAY 5: THE CROSS 39

DAY 6: FAITH 47

DAY 7: PRAYER 52

DAY 8: SPIRITUAL GIFTS 61

DAY 9: LEND A HAND..66

DAY 10: WITNESSING 74

DAY 11: WHO YOU ARE 80

DAY 12: HISTORY 87

DAY 13: THE HEART..91

DAY 14: REPENTANCE..98

DAY 15: HOLINESS...103

DAY 16: JUDGMENT...111

DAY 17: JESUS'S RETURN..116

DAY 18: SACRAMENTS..123

DAY 19: SPIRITUAL LAW 128

DAY 20: NUMBER ONE!..135

DAY 21: INCREASING 141

BOOKS OF THE BIBLE IN ORDER............................148

CHRISTIAN LINGO..150

NAMES OF GOD IN THE BIBLE....................................156

RECOMMENDED BOOKS OR MATERIALS............160

MORE RECOMMENDED BOOKS 172

SPECIAL THANKS..174

ABOUT THE AUTHORS 177

INTRODUCTION

Welcome! If you have asked Jesus to be the Lord of your life, then you have before you a whole new world of possibilities! This book is designed to help you get started. If you have received this book and have not given your life to God, then you can do that by asking Jesus to be your Lord and submitting your life to Him. There is no magical formula. Just talk to Him. Check out Romans 10:9 (chapter 10, verse 9) in the Bible for more help or talk to whoever gave you this book.

For the next twenty-one days, you will learn and experience incredible things! Each day contains a different "mini" lesson. I say "mini" because there is a lot more to learn about each topic. For further study, check out the "Recommended Materials" in the back of the book. If needed, purchase a Bible like a

New American Standard, New King James, English Standard, or New International Version Bible.

Each lesson contains a place for "two-way journaling." This is explained on day one. I highly recommend that you do this every day, because it places in your hands a way to connect with God. We need to connect with God more than anything! Don't settle to simply read the material. Do the journaling. You may be surprised by what happens. *Also, take time to look up the verses in the text. It will help you become familiar with the Bible.*

At the end of each lesson, you will find a question that I pose to you. There is also a place for you to write down questions of your own. Take your questions to a trusted friend like your pastor or a spiritual mentor. Seeing someone once a week is a good way to learn. Get their opinions on your answers and see if they can answer your questions. Christianity is a journey, not a destination, and these questions will help you along that journey.

At the end of the book, you will find some extra "helps." These are pages with things I thought might help. For example, there is a page on "Christian Lingo." These are words and phrases you may hear that you have not heard before. Check those pages out too.

Some people say that it takes twenty-one days to start a new habit. I hope to help you start a new habit of connecting with God! Enjoy!

—*Benjamin Williams*

 # DAY 1:
VOICE OF GOD

At its core, one of the most important aspects of Christianity is having a relationship with God. This is why I feel it is very important to begin this book with the subject of how to hear God's voice. You may be surprised to learn that God actually wants to talk to you. Jesus affirmed this truth when He said, "My sheep (followers) hear My voice," and again when He said that eternal life was really about knowing Him (John 10:27, John 17:3, parenthesis added).

God speaks in many ways. Job 33:14 says, "For God does speak-now one way, now another-though man may not perceive it (NIV). He speaks through the Bible, dreams, visions, angels, circumstances, His audible voice, nature, other people, intuition, and other ways. It will help you to study these ways in more depth. I highly recommend doing a separate study on dream interpretation, since dreams are a very common way that God speaks (Job 33:14–15). In this lesson, I want to introduce you to a simple way to hear from God. It is called, "two-way journaling" and is a great place to start. As you mature, you will be able to build off of this.

Two-way journaling is asking God a question and writing down what you believe He has told you in response. I have provided a place for two-way journaling at the end of each lesson. Please journal every day. He wants to speak with you more than you want to hear His voice. So you can journal and then take your journaling to a trusted friend, mentor, or pastor for them to review. Allow them to help you and don't be worried about being a little off. Just keep journaling. You are growing! Some people are so afraid of being wrong that they don't even give hearing from God a chance. Hebrews 5:14 states, "but solid food is for the mature, who by constant use have trained themselves to distinguish good from evil." God's plan for you to become accurate in knowing whether something is from Him is through regular practice. Make it a practice to do what I am teaching you in this lesson and your ability to hear from God will grow strong and accurate. Here are four key ideas to help you get started.

- Key # 1: Spontaneity
- Key # 2: Stillness
- Key # 3: Vision
- Key # 4: Journaling

All right, let's look at Key # 1: Spontaneity.

One way God speaks is from the inside of you! Why? Because He has come to live in you as shown in 1 Corinthians 6:19. It states, "or do you not know that your body is a temple of the Holy Spirit who is in you…" God's voice inside of you is commonly called "God's still small voice." And what it sounds like is a thought. Not just any thought but a spontaneous thought that is wiser and more loving than your normal thoughts. You may be driving somewhere and someone's face comes to mind, and you know that you are supposed to pray for them. That is God! So, pray! It is not forced but spontaneous. This means that you don't work at forcing yourself to hear from God but position yourself to hear from Him. We will apply this knowledge in a minute.

Key # 2: Stillness.

If you are anxious or busy thinking about worrisome issues, then it will be difficult to listen for the voice of God. Begin by sitting in a comfortable position and closing your eyes. Focus your heart on Jesus. Maybe sing to Him quietly or just say his name over and over until you feel yourself relax. This is a good mental place to be to hear from God. The Bible tells us that, "Jesus often withdrew to lonely places and prayed" (Luke 5:16). Find a quite place and put your attention on Jesus.

After you are still, you will want to apply Key # 3: Vision.

When you read the word "tree," what comes to mind? The letters? Or a picture of a tree? Why? We think in pictures. God designed us this way on purpose. A lot can be communicated through pictures as someone once said, "a picture is worth a thousand words." The imagination can be used for evil or it can be used for good. For example Psalms 2:1 states, "why do the people rage, and why do the people imagine a vain thing" (KJV). But Joshua 1:8 contains a command from God, "this Book of the Law shall not depart from your mouth, but you shall meditate on it day and night" (NKJV). The word "meditate" in Joshua is the same word translated "imagine" in Psalms. See Strong's Concordance Hebrew # 1897. In one Scripture the imagination is being used for evil and one is the imagination being used for good as the people imagined the Book of the Law or what we would call the Bible. We want to be people that offer our imaginations as a platform for the voice of God.

This is one way that God speaks. An easy way to start this is to read a story about Jesus in the books of Matthew, Mark, Luke, or John (the Gospels). Close your eyes and place yourself in the story. Then come to Jesus and ask Him a question. Don't plan it out. Just ask and allow Jesus to speak to you. Allowing Jesus to speak for Himself without imagining what He would say is the spontaneous thoughts mentioned in Key # 1. Later you may not need to picture something to hear from God, but this is a good way to start and provides a focal point for the time set aside to hear from God so your attention does not wander away from hearing from God to tasks that need to be done.

The book of Daniel has many references to pictures in the mind. Most books in the Bible speak about visions but the book of Daniel clarifies that many of the visions Daniel had were in the platform of the imagination. Ephesians 1:18 calls the imagination "the eyes of your heart." Refer to Daniel 7:1 for a reference to God speaking to someone with pictures in his mind.

Finally, you will want to write down what God tells you. This is Key # 4: Journaling.

Basically, the whole Bible contains the two-way journal entries of people that sought God. What you hear from God in your journaling does not replace the Bible and should not go against what is taught in the Bible, but it will lead you to greater intimacy with God.

God is smart and can help you in many areas. He is not just for church services but is relevant in all aspects of life. Two-way journaling is a way to invite Him into those areas.

It is also important for you to know that, at times, God does not speak in plain speech. Just as Jesus spoke using stories, at times God will speak with pictures and phrases that are not obvious. The purpose of this is not to confuse you but to invite you to discover the meaning with God and your friends. It is an invitation into a relationship. "It is the glory of God to conceal a matter, but the glory of kings to search out a matter" (Proverbs 25:2). God speaks in a variety of ways. As you grow in your relationship with God, you will discover that hearing His voice is a fun adventure!

If you want more information, you can look up Mark Virkler, CWGministries.org. On that website, you will find an in-depth look at the four keys as well as how those keys come from the Bible passage Habakkuk 2:1–2 which states,

> "I will stand on my guard post and station myself on the rampart; and I will keep watch to see what He will speak to me, and how I reply when I reproved. 2. Then the Lord answered me and said, 'Record the vision and inscribe it on tablets, that the one who reads it may run.'"

Let's begin two-way journaling now, because it really is one of the best ways to learn about God. Take a minute and read John chapter 1.

Picture yourself in John 1:35–51. Then afterward come and sit next to Jesus. Ask Him one of the following questions.

1. What do you think about me?
2. Do you love me?

I highly recommend staying away from questions like "Why did Dad die?" You may hear answers to emotionally sensitive questions later, but for now, keep it simple. Write what Jesus says to you on the provided lines. Remember: still yourself, picture the scene, ask Jesus a question, and write down what He says back to you.

_____

_____

_____

_____

_____

_____

Here is a place for you to write down any questions you have that came up while reading this lesson. Take your questions to a person of spiritual maturity that you trust.

Question: How important do you think it is to hear God's voice?

DAY 2:
THE KINGDOM

While the subject of the kingdom of heaven is immense and, in fact, touches on all areas of life, I will provide for you some basic information. That being said, it may be one of the most important subjects that you study further. It is a simple concept with complex applications. You can refer to the "Recommended Books" for a list of books for further study.

The disciples of Jesus asked Him to teach them how to pray. He provided an outlined prayer that many have come to call "The Lord's Prayer" (Matthew 6:9–13). This prayer holds in a nutshell the message of the kingdom. Jesus said to pray to God the Father: "Your kingdom come. Your will be done on earth as it is in heaven."

You can see how this works when you read that Jesus said when the kingdom got near someone, they were physically healed or set free from demons (Matthew 4:23, 12:28). He also taught that in the kingdom there is all the provision we need for everything in life (Matthew 6:33). Why? Are there sick people in heaven? No. Are there demons tormenting people in heaven? No. Is there lack of provision, food, clothing, or shelter in heaven? No. So, when His kingdom comes and His will is done here as it is in heaven, then what it is like in heaven occurs here.

So, what is the desire of God for the earth? For it to reflect heaven. It is for His ways and the ways of His kingdom to be shown to all people. How is this done? Through you and me! Jesus said that the kingdom of God is in you (Luke 17:21). There is a real place called heaven, but you as a follower of Christ can release heaven here on earth! You can become the vehicle through which the prayer of Jesus Christ is answered.

Ask God to begin showing you how to release His kingdom through your life. He may tell you to pray for someone at, for example, a grocery store, or He may tell you how to run your business better. Most likely, He will tell you both and much more.

In giving your life to Jesus, you switched kingdoms. You were in the kingdom of darkness, and now you are in the kingdom of light (Colossians 1:12–13). As His follower, you are now called to release His kingdom so darkness is pushed back. God is not interested only in you just making it to heaven one day. He wants you to bring heaven to earth right now as well!

While this lesson is *very* simplistic, it does give the basic message Jesus preached and that you can live out. You are a laborer together with Christ, living to display the love, wisdom, and power of God's ways to anyone in your area of influence. Release His kingdom in your home, in your school, in your workplace, and to the hurting people all around you. As you do, you will see miracles happen. This is the gospel of the kingdom, which is shown not only through words but also through demonstrations of power. Matthew 4:23 states,

> "Jesus was going through all Galilee, teaching in their synagogues and proclaiming the

gospel of the kingdom, and healing every kind of disease and every kind of sickness among the people. 1 Corinthians 4:20 emphasizes the truth Jesus modeled, "for the kingdom of God does not consist in words but in power."

Read John chapter 2. Still yourself and place yourself in John 2:1–11. Come to Jesus and ask Him one of these questions:

1. What does your kingdom look like?

2. How do I release light?

_____

_____

_____

_____

_____

_____

_____

Here is a place for you to write down any questions you have that came up while reading this lesson. Take your questions to a person of spiritual maturity that you trust.

Question: Why is God interested in earth reflecting heaven?

 # DAY 3: BELONGING

Someone once asked me if they could be a Christian and not go to church. "Perhaps," I told her, "but it would be similar to you cutting off your finger and claiming it was still a part of your body. It is still a finger, but it is not receiving the life and nourishment it needs for growth and to function to its full potential." You see, when you gave your life to Christ, you were joined with what the Bible calls the body of Christ (1 Corinthians 12:27). We were designed to be connected with people. Doing this helps promote spiritual maturity.

God not only received you to Himself, but also called you to be in His family (John 1:12). The Bible even says to "not forsake the assembling together of the saints (or followers of Christ)" (see Hebrews 10:25, parenthesis added). Are you a part of a local church? If not, then you will be like that finger cut off from the body. You will not mature in a healthy manner without being with other believers.

I need to take it one step further. When Jesus called the disciples, He told them to follow Him (Mark 1:17). They were in a close relationship with the one that taught them. This is a good picture for maturing spiritually. It would greatly benefit you to find someone to mentor you in spiritual matters. This may be someone you take your journal entries to or someone you meet with to ask questions or even someone you just hang around that you know is more spiritually mature than you are. It is when you are in a close relationship with a spiritual mentor that Jesus can "make you" into something more than you could be alone (Mark 1:17).

Don't know anyone that can help? Talk to your pastor. Don't have a church? You can look up churches in your phone book. You can ask people you work with or you can go online to www.globalawakening.com and look up affiliated churches. Look for a church that teaches Jesus, practices healing the sick, teaches on the kingdom and believes that the church is called to be a victorious church at the return of Christ, and you will probably be in a good place. Whatever you do, *get connected!* I cannot overstate how important it is for you to not just go to church but to also be involved in a relationship with spiritually mature people.

Starting relationships with spiritually mature people takes vulnerability and trust, but I can tell you, it is worth it. It may save your life. God works through people, and He wants to use others to encourage and challenge you as well as you doing the same for them. Remember, who you hang around will influence who you become!

I should include here that personal relationships are not the only way to be mentored. While you should never cut off personal relationships, you can also be mentored by people through books, CDs, messages online, etcetera. Spend a lot of time with God, with people, and with mentors from afar, and you will be amazed at how fast you begin to mature spiritually.

Read John chapter 3. Still yourself and place yourself in John 3:1–2. Come to Jesus and ask Him one of these questions:

1. What does it look like to belong to you?
2. How do I trust people?

Here is a place for you to write down any questions you have that came up while reading this lesson. Take your questions to a person of spiritual maturity that you trust.

_____

_____

_____

Question: How can you get to know people in your church?

_____

_____

_____

# DAY 4:
THE BIBLE

Why do people read the Bible? Is it really needed? If you miss this lesson, you will end up spiritually weak and easily misled into believing false ideas. The Bible is the disclosure of God's heart for humanity. Without it, there would be no standard for truth or reality from the perspective of God.

Think about this. The way we know how fast something is moving is by comparing it to an unmoving object. This is one way that the Bible works. Societies change, but the Bible remains the same. It is a good practice to always check out what the Bible says about a matter. It is the number-one authority. Hold it higher than any sermon you hear, any book you read, any journal entry you write, and any prophecy (defined in back of book) you receive. The Bible is *the* standard; it is God's voice on paper.

(Matthew 24:35, "Heaven and earth will pass away, but my words will not pass away").

Not only is the Bible the standard, but it is also spiritual food (1 Corinthians 3:1–2). Just as your body needs nourishment to sustain its life, so your spirit needs the Bible to sustain spiritual life. However, I must give a caution here. It is not the Bible in and of itself that gives spiritual nourishment to people. Some read the Bible and do not believe it, so it does nothing for them. It is when you combine reading with faith (belief followed by action) that the Bible's power is released.

Some people make the mistake of reading the Bible as a static book. In other words, to them it is a book with history that has little to do with their everyday lives. When it is combined with principles, it can be a powerful tool used by God to speak to you. Let's take a look at some of these principles. For the sake of space, this is brief, so check out some of the recommended books to help you go deeper in this subject.

There are many principles that people have come up with to help with reading the Bible. Here are three. They are context, revelation, and friends. These will help protect you and provide a platform for a genuine relationship with God. In real estate, there are three things that are key: location, location, location. The same is true when you approach reading the Bible. This "location" is called *context*. Context is looking at the "location" or the "where is it?" of what is in the Bible. This has two basic applications. One is to understand the culture in which it was written. The second is to find how a particular verse relates to the verses around it. In other words, what is the author trying to communicate to the original recipients in its original setting? When someone from America reads the Bible, they may not understand a verse in the same way someone in the Middle East 2,000 years ago would have understood it.

Some tools that will help you understand the original recipients are Bible dictionaries and Bible commentaries. Another method to understanding the context of a particular verse is to read the surrounding verses. Typically, Bibles have verses grouped together in paragraphs, which are called passages. Remember though, the Bible is more like a letter than a book. So, the context of a verse may extend to a previous and/or later chapter.

As you are reading the Bible, you will want to ask God to speak to you. One way God will speak to you when you are reading the Bible is you may have a verse that "jumps out at you." This is when your attention seems drawn to a certain verse or it is as if you understand it for the first time even though you have read it before. When a verse seems to jump out at you is when the Bible becomes interactive. Hebrews 4:12 states, "For the word of God is living and active ..." God never intended the Bible to be reduced to a history book, a book about morality, or a book of principles for living. While the Bible does include those things and they are important, the design of God is that through the Bible His voice is alive and interactive in our lives. This is where God is emphasizing something to you while you are reading. He could be emphasizing an area that He wants changed in your life or He could be helping you understand Him and how He thinks, operates, and feels.

I often compare this to something that used to happen on old cartoons. Have you seen an old cartoon where a character gets an idea and a light bulb appears above their head and turns on? This is a picture of something jumping out at you while reading the Bible. It is as if the light came on. The Bible calls this "revelation." This is where God helps you understand something important or "reveals" it to you. Ephesians 1:17 calls for the need for "revelation in the knowledge of Him." I am not talking about the book in the Bible called "Revelation" but rather a supernatural understanding that only God can give. Jesus gave an example of receiving revelation knowledge when He told a guy that no one on earth had helped him understand that Jesus is who He said He was but Father God had revealed it to Him (Matthew 16:17). You know it has happened when a verse "becomes yours" or seems to "make sense." It is no longer what someone else has said, but it is your very own understanding. This will happen often as you listen for God to speak to you, and it should be your pursuit in reading the Bible. Don't make the mistake of reading the Bible to be able to argue with others. Read the Bible to encounter God, to hear His voice.

Finally, as you are reading the Bible and God is speaking to you, there is one other thing to keep in mind: friends. By this I mean two things. One is that, when you believe that God has shown you something in the Bible, see if there are other verses (friends) that say the same thing. Never build an idea off of just one verse. The other is that it is always wise to submit things to friends you trust. These friends can help support you in understanding the truth. It is good to take both journal entries as well as what you believe God showed you in the Bible to friends. Together you will mature.

I encourage you to read the entire Bible. God will refer to the Bible when He speaks to you, so it is good to have read it all. Refer to the back of this book for help. I recommend one of these Bible versions: New American Standard, New King James, New International Version, or English Standard Version.

Read John chapter 4. Still yourself and place yourself in John 4:5–6. Come to Jesus at the well and ask Him one of these questions:

1. How important is the Bible?
2. How do I read the Bible with you?

Here is a place for you to write down any questions you have that came up while reading this lesson. Take your questions to a person of spiritual maturity that you trust.

_____

_____

_____

Question: What things are standing out to you as you read the book of John?

_____

_____

_____

DAY 5:
THE CROSS

So what's the big deal about the cross? You've seen crosses above church buildings and on necklaces, but why? The cross is central to the Christian faith because it is the gateway back to God's original plan for humanity. This original plan was for intimacy with God and dominion on the earth.

If you are not familiar with the story of creation, take a minute to read Genesis 1–3. This records briefly how God created the world and the first humans, Adam and Eve. These two were created in God's image and after God's likeness, which is unique to humanity compared to everything else that God created. They were given a mandate to be fruitful, multiply, and subdue or take dominion over the earth.

They began existence as beings in God's image. This means that humanity carries in it aspects of what God is like. Being made in God's image also implies that we were created for intimacy with God. While some may disagree, I believe that you cannot have the depth of relationship with an animal that you can with a human. Why? Because animals are not in our image. We were created in God's image to reflect Him on earth, and so that we could have intimacy with Him.

As beings created in God's image, Adam and Eve were given instructions. They were "in charge" on the earth. Have you ever wondered about why, if God wanted us to be with Him, He created us on earth and not in heaven? It is because He wanted us to have our own place (Psalms 115:16). Adam and Eve originally had authority over the earth, but when they gave into the devil's temptation, they gave that authority to him.

This is where all hope seemed to be lost. God had given Adam and Eve authority, and they gave it away (Luke 4:5–6). Fortunately, God was not surprised and had a plan. The plan was simple yet profound. All He had to do was to provide a way for people to come back to Him. The answer was to have someone come under the penalty of death that did not deserve to die, someone who had not sinned (done anything wrong). But there was no one. All have sinned (Romans 3:23).

So God did the unthinkable. He came Himself. The Bible tells us that there is one God (Mark 12:32). This one God is made up of the Father, the Son (Jesus), and the Holy Spirit, called the *Trinity*. How? I don't fully understand. But it may be like an egg. It has an eggshell, an egg yoke, and egg white—three parts, but all one egg. It is simplistic but a good picture. If you look up Luke 3:21–22, you will see all three: Jesus getting baptized, the Father speaking, and the Spirit coming upon Jesus. You may also refer to John 10:30, which shows that Jesus and the Father are one, and Romans 8:9 to see that the Holy Spirit is also called "the Spirit of Christ."

According to Philippians 2:6–7, Jesus emptied Himself and walked the earth as a human. He was 100 percent God and 100 percent man. He lived a sinless life and died on the cross (Philippians 2:7). His unjust death on our behalf broke open a means for the restoration of God's original design, this being intimacy with Him, multiplying (leading people to Christ), and taking dominion (releasing heaven on earth). Acts 3:21 says, "(Jesus) whom heaven must receive until the period of restoration of all things about which God spoke by the mouth of His holy prophets from ancient time." Through Jesus things are being restored to God's original plan which is ultimately completed at the return of Christ.

Without Jesus dying on the cross, we would be without hope, but the whole world is reconciled to God by His death (Ephesians 2:12–13, 1 John 2:2). The reference in Ephesians says, "remember that you were at that time separate from Christ, excluded from the commonwealth of Israel, and strangers to covenants of promise, having no hope and without God in the world. But now in Christ Jesus you who formerly were far off have been brought near by the blood of Christ." Now the world has to receive Him as their Lord. It is because He died that we can be forgiven of sins (Hebrews 9:22, "and according to the Law, one may almost say, all things are cleansed with blood, and without shedding of blood there is no forgiveness"). It is because of His death that we can be healed (1 Peter 2:24). First Peter says, "and He Himself (Jesus) bore our sins in His body on the cross, so that we might die to sin and live to righteousness; for by His wounds you were healed." Since He died, we have the provision of heaven (2 Corinthians 8:9, Ephesians 4:19). It is because of the cross that we can receive the Holy Spirit (John 16:7). Everything that we need in life is found in discovering what His sacrifice has provided for us (2 Peter 1:3, "seeing that His divine power has granted to us everything pertaining to life and godliness, through the true knowledge of Him who called us by His own glory and excellence").

This is not a movie. It is better! Since He died unjustly, He destroyed the power of death and was resurrected! Without the resurrection, our belief would be in vain (1 Corinthians 15:14). But since we serve a living, risen King, we have access to a relationship with Him and access to what He has provided in His kingdom!

What Jesus accomplished by His death and resurrection is beyond words (2 Corinthians 9:15). He died so that we could enter into what was destroyed in the beginning. Some people thank God for the cross but never access more than forgiveness and eternal life. This is a great tragedy, since He paid such a high price for much more. You will honor Jesus's death and resurrection by pursuing all that His sacrifice has provided. Search in the Bible what has been done for you and honor Jesus by going aggressively after all that His sacrifice has provided. He is a rewarder of those that diligently seek Him (Hebrews 11:6).

Lastly, perhaps one of most important things to not miss in relation to God is that He thinks in covenant terms. A covenant is a binding agreement sealed in blood. It is eternal and unbreakable. People try to compare it to a legal contract, but it is much more than that. It is a blood agreement to be allies. That is why, in Romans 8:31, the Bible states, "if God is for us, who can be against us?" You have a blood covenant with God through the death of Jesus! All of heaven backs up this covenant.

While what I have said is all true, there is more. The death and resurrection of Jesus goes beyond the original design. The cross takes us to the place where we are more than what Adam and Eve were. The Bible tells us that we become a "new creation," where God lives in us and has joined Himself to our spirit (see 2 Corinthians 5:17 and 1 Corinthians 6:17). You are a new breed of person God dreamed up before He created the world, and the cross made this relationship available. That is the power of the cross!

Read John chapter 5. Still yourself and place yourself in John 5:2–3. Come to Jesus at the pool and ask Him one of these questions:

1. What did the cross release for me?
2. How do I apply the power of the cross?

_____

_____

_____

_____

_____

_____

_____

_____

_____

_____

Here is a place for you to write down any questions you have that came up while reading this lesson. Take your questions to a person of spiritual maturity that you trust.

Question: What happens if we stay at the cross rejoicing in forgiveness and never go through the cross to the other provisions?

# DAY 6: FAITH

Faith, according to the Bible, is, "the assurance of things hoped for and the evidence of things not seen" (Hebrews 11:1). What you can understand from this verse is that faith looks like confidence and provides proof of something intangible. With a little mixture of confidence in hope and proof of what cannot be seen with the natural eye, you have faith. Today's lesson is to help clarify that definition and to assist you with tools to strengthen your faith.

To have faith, according to the Bible, you need to have hope first. *Hope*, in relation to God, is understanding His revealed will. We have the hope of salvation (1 Thessalonians 5:8), but we do not have the hope to be, for example, the color green. Why? Because it is not the revealed will of God. As you read the Bible, you will recognize things that God desires for you. As you do, you will feel hope rising in your heart. While that is a good start, it is not the end of it.

Your hope must lead to proof for it to be faith. It is not enough to say that you believe in Jesus. You must also live for Him for it to be true faith (James 2:14–24). Let me give a simple illustration. You can say that you believe (hope) a chair will hold you up, but you prove that you have faith in that chair's ability by sitting down on it.

Do you have hope that God speaks to us? Then listen. Do you have hope that God heals people? Then pray for the sick. You begin at the revealed will of God. As you have hope that God actually does have a certain thing in mind for you, then act in obedience to that hope. When you do that, faith is born! Faith is what releases the revealed will of God to be done on earth (Matthew 9:29).

Faith is the best way that we can bring pleasure to God (Hebrew 11:6). Everything we do will show if we have faith or not. Simply said, faith is trusting God and proving it. He loves for His children to show that they trust Him. So hold on tight to your confession of faith (Hebrews 4:14). Show God that you have faith in what was accomplished by the death and resurrection of Jesus Christ. Show Him by your trust and show Him with your actions. One way to increase your faith is to increase your knowledge of the revealed will of God. Increase your hope, and you will increase your faith. Understanding the revealed will of God comes through reading the Bible with the Holy Spirit. Two-way journaling and talking to friends about what you read is a good way to do this. Faith comes by hearing and hearing by the word (*rhema*) of God (Romans 10:17).

This lifetime is all the opportunity you have to offer to God the gift of a life of faith. Let me put this in perspective for you. You do not have faith for what you see (Romans 8:24). One day you will live without faith. You will have access to walk with Jesus in a physical relationship that is unparalleled to anything anyone has experienced so far. As far as I know this earthly life is the only timeframe where we will be able to live by faith. This life is it! This is the only chance you have to offer to God a life of faith that will bring Him pleasure throughout all eternity. Offer your life to Him. Count it an honor to live by faith so that you can bring your King great joy. What this means is that at times God will provide a platform for you to live by faith and bring

Him pleasure in a way that cannot be duplicated in eternity. So, as you face a circumstance you don't understand or feel God wants you to do something that does not make sense, know that it is an opportunity to trust God and demonstrate your faith in Him by not giving up and by choosing to be obedient. It will not last forever. This is your shot at living a life of faith! His quest is to find a people full of faith (Luke 18:8). Will He find you as a person of faith?

Read John chapter 6. Still yourself and place yourself in John 6:1–15. Come to Jesus at the mountain and ask Him one of these questions:

    1. How do I personally increase my faith?

    2. How do you see my level of faith?

Here is a place for you to write down any questions you have that came up while reading this lesson. Take your questions to a person of spiritual maturity that you trust.

_____

_____

_____

Question: Read Matthew 7:21–23. What does faith have to do with obedience?

_____

_____

_____

 # DAY 7: PRAYER

Prayer is communicating with God. More than anything in the world, God wants a relationship with you. His desire is not simply that you make it to heaven instead of hell. Jesus died so that you can *know* Him (John 17:3, "this is eternal life, that they may know you the only true God, and Jesus Christ whom you have sent").

While there are no formulas, there are some things that might help you in developing a relationship with God. Remember, the number one thing you need to do is to connect with God in prayer. It is hard to describe, but you will know it when it happens. As you pursue Him in prayer, God promises that you will find Him (Jeremiah 29:13). What an astounding thought! The Almighty Creator has made Himself so vulnerable that He allows people to touch His heart. God has promised that if you really want to, you can truly know Him! One of the ways you will get to know God is through prayer.

Although praying is about connecting with God and not punching in a time clock, it is still good to start with some ideas. It is kind of like doing some type of marriage enrichment. Anyone who has experienced the benefits of learning how to communicate better with their spouse knows that relationships can get better with certain techniques. The techniques are designed to enhance the relationship, not replace it. This same principle applies to prayer. The end result is a relationship. Never allow the end result to be prayer itself. Make an effort at different ways of praying and see which ones help you to connect with God the best.

I will provide for you some ways that people pray. Your prayer life will change over time, and that is good. Utilize each type of prayer style I provide a few times. You can even mix them together or just do part of one. These are not the only ways to pray, but they do help in facilitating a relationship.

One way that many people feel helps them to connect with God is by singing to Him. You may hear this commonly called *worship*. If you play an instrument, you can use that, or if you are like me and can only play the radio, then a CD or MP3 player can help. Play an instrument or put some music on and sing to Him. The Bible tells us that God loves this (Psalm 22:3). You may encounter God's presence powerfully as you sing to Him.

Another way people like to pray is commonly called *soaking*. This dates back to Samuel lying before the presence of God (1 Samuel 3:2). It is what it sounds like, lying before God. Put some music on and come to just be with Him. Tell Him that you are not asking anything from Him. You just want to hang out. You may receive visions in your mind (Daniel 4:5), visions outside your body (Ezekiel 1:1), a strong peace, the voice of God, or any number of things. Many powerful encounters have happened as people have done this. Pursuing God is never wasted time!

Another type of prayer is called the *ripple method.* It is utilizing the idea of tossing a pebble in a body of water and causing ripples. The first splash is praying for yourself, and then every other ripple is praying for someone farther and farther away from yourself relationally. For example, after praying for yourself, you may pray for your family and then your co-workers and so on.

People also use outlines. The outline may be a passage of Scripture. For example, some may use the Lord's Prayer (Matthew 6:9–13). They would not pray the prayer word for word but use each line as a spring board to pray about what the verse states. So, someone may begin thanking God for being their heavenly Father and focus on what the implications are, like God loving them unconditionally, as a good father would. You can use the apostle's prayers found in the book of Acts and in the other books called Epistles (one example is Ephesians 1:15–21). You may also consider using chapters in the book of Psalms. Some people use the verses on the armor of God (Ephesians 6:11) or the tabernacle (Hebrews 8:5) as outlines. Outlines are good because they keep you focused and moving forward.

People who want to pray regularly for particular people or things can also make a list. This is really good for natural list makers. Write down who or what you want to pray about and pray down the list. The only caution I have with this idea is that it can easily lead to prayer being the end result. Always incorporate hearing God's voice and the presence of God to help protect you from dry prayer times. Expect God to speak to you and expect to feel His presence. If you do not experience this during prayer, then consider it a game of hide and go seek. God is hiding because He wants you to pursue Him (Hebrews 11:6B, "He is a rewarder of those that seek him"). He is a good father, and you should expect good things from Him (James 1:17).

Since this subject is a big one, please allow me to end with a jumble of last thoughts. I encourage you to pray out loud. It helps keep your mind from wandering. Many people find saying the promises of God out loud is a powerful prayer tool (look at "Recommended Books" for a book on this). Allow God to lead you. He may lead you to do different things in prayer. Maybe He will tell you who to pray for or tell you to write Him a poem or dance or shout or paint. It is good to pray alone and with others. Finally, praying in other tongues can help. Praying in tongues is a gift of God where people speak to God in another language that could be an earthly language or a language of angels (1 Corinthians 13:1).

These languages are not learned but come through an experience with God (Acts 2:4, "and they were all filled with the Holy Spirit and began to speak with other tongues, as the Spirit was giving them utterance"). When we pray tongues we speak to God in a language that we do not understand, but God does and He causes us to be spiritually strengthened. First Corinthians 14:2, 4A states, "for one who speaks in a tongue does not speak to men but to God; for no one understands, but in his spirit he speaks mysteries. One who speaks in a tongue edifies himself." Ask the leadership at your church about receiving this gift. Remember it is about having a relationship with God. You will be fine. And it will be fun!

Prayer life examples:

1. In the morning, pour a cup of coffee and put on a worship CD. Sit with God, allowing Him to love on you (soaking). Read the Bible, two-way journal, pray, and sing love songs to God.

2. Set a timer for five minutes and go down a list of twelve names or needs. Spend five minutes on each name or need, and before

you will know it, you will have prayed for an hour.

3. Present to God a journal where you dialogue with God about various topics. These can be topics focused on your curiosity, responsibility or on getting to know Him.

4. Do a search of promises in the Bible and write them down. Then go to the promises and speak them out loud, declaring your trust in God. Incorporate speaking in tongues.

5. Put on worship music and imagine yourself in a certain region of the world. Then dance before God inviting Him into that area of the world.

6. Lay before God and focus your attention on Him. Bring to Him your heart and abandon yourself to Him. Keep focused on Him until you feel released to go.

7. Present yourself before God to worship Him with no requests. Ask for nothing. Simply love on Him with singing, silence, or whatever expression of love rises in your heart.

8. Go to Ephesians chapter one and pray through each verse.

Read John chapter 7. Still yourself and place yourself in John 7:37–39. Come to Jesus and ask Him one of these questions:

1. How do you see prayer?
2. What do you want from me in prayer?

Here is a place for you to write down any questions you have that came up while reading this lesson. Take your questions to a person of spiritual maturity that you trust.

_____

_____

_____

Question: What does prayer have to do with everyday life?

_____

_____

_____

DAY 8:
SPIRITUAL GIFTS

God is all powerful and can do anything. But most of all "God is love" and this powerful God enjoys demonstrating His love powerfully (1 John 4:8). One of the ways He does this is by giving us spiritual gifts. These gifts are not for showing us off or for any selfish gain but to show off the love of God to hurting and needy people. I say this because these gifts are beyond human ability. They are powerful. Some have even wanted to pay to receive them (Acts 8:18). But gifts cannot be bought!

These gifts can only be received and then used to help others. The gifts come from the Holy Spirit and are actually packaged in receiving Him. Various churches believe different things about receiving the Holy Spirit. Some call it being baptized in the Holy Spirit, while others call it receiving the fullness of the Spirit. Still others call it actualizing the Spirit, and others say it is simply receiving the second half of the first blessing. Confusing, huh? It would be worthwhile for you to ask your pastor the beliefs of your church, to talk to God about it, and to read the recommended books. A good foundation is built by knowing that God gives the Spirit to all who ask (Luke 11:13) and reading the first two chapters in the book of Acts.

Some of these spiritual gifts can be found in 1 Corinthians 12. God is not limited to these gifts, but the list provides the more common ones. It would be impossible for me to expound on all the gifts here. The main purpose for this lesson is to expose you to them and encourage you to ask God for all of them, especially for the gift of prophesy (1 Corinthians 14:1). This gift touches people deeper than the others.

People consider the "least" of the gifts that of speaking in other tongues. This is not meant to imply that you do not need this gift, but it is called this because it is the only gift focused on yourself (Jude 1:20). All the other gifts are intended to benefit others. I believe that all should pray in tongues (1 Corinthians 14:18, 39); however, if you only speak in tongues and are not motivated out of love to use the other gifts to help people, then your speaking in tongues has little value before God (if you think I'm too harsh, then read 1 Corinthians 13).

As you pursue these gifts, pay attention around you and to what is happening in you to develop them. For example, at first, you may think a pain in your body is actually just you, but it may be a "word of knowledge" of a pain in someone else's body. Reading books on how God has used these gifts in others is a good way to learn how to operate in these gifts. I have seen it time and time again that as people learn about how God has worked through others they themselves begin to see more of these gifts operating in their own lives. If you have people around you that are operating in these gifts then ask if you can go with and watch.

While pursuing these gifts, don't be afraid to make a mistake. You are growing, and we all make mistakes when we are learning. The more you use the gift the more the gift will grow and mature. Frankly, one of the most exciting things is to operate in the gifts of the Spirit! Don't miss out!

Read John chapter 8. Still yourself and place yourself in John 8:1–11. Come to Jesus after verse 11 and ask Him one of these questions:

1. What spiritual gifts have you already given me?
2. What spiritual gift do you want me to pursue?

Here is a place for you to write down any questions you have that came up while reading this lesson. Take your questions to a person of spiritual maturity that you trust.

_____

_____

_____

Question: Why does God give us spiritual gifts?

_____

_____

_____

DAY 9:
LEND A HAND

One of the biblical teachings considered to be "elementary" is the "laying on of hands" (Hebrew 6:1–2). Since it is so foundational, I want to explore the power of "laying on of hands" in this lesson.

God does not explain everything in the Bible. For example, the Bible states that there is no forgiveness of sin without the shedding of blood (Hebrews 9:22). Why? I honestly do not know. However, it is a serious enough condition for Jesus to have to shed blood for us! God does not explain why, but in many places, it can be seen in the Bible the fact that power is released through the "laying on of hands."

When the Bible tells of God's hand being upon someone, it means His power through His Spirit is coming upon someone (2 Kings 3:15). Since we are created in His image, it should be no surprise that power can come through us laying our hand on someone (Acts 28:8). Simply said, this is the power of the Holy Spirit coming through our hands and touching someone else.

The Bible shows three basic outcomes in the "laying on of hands." One is impartation. A second is receiving the Holy Spirit. And the third is physical healing. Each one of these outcomes has two parts.

Impartation is taking of the Spirit that is on someone's life and putting it on someone else. Sound crazy? That is exactly what God told Moses that He was going to do with him (Numbers 11:17). There are two parts to impartation. One is to give a spiritual gift to someone (1 Timothy 4:14). The other is to release a blessing to someone that is recognized as having been called by God for specific ministry (Acts 13:1–3). Impartation through the laying on of hands can release a gift of the Spirit or enhance spiritual activity in someone's ministry, but it must not be done lightly (1 Timothy 5:22). This is because we are expected to use what has been entrusted to us (Matthew 25:19). So do not receive the laying on of hands for impartation without first resolving to use what is given to you!

One of the ways to receive the Holy Spirit is to have someone lay hands on you. This can be seen in the Bible over and over (Acts 8:17, 19:6). If you want to receive the Holy Spirit, you can ask someone at your church to lay hands on you and pray for this.

However, this is not the only meaning of receiving the Holy Spirit. I cannot really point it out in the Bible, but I can tell you from experience that many people feel the presence of God when someone lays their hand on them and prays for them. Not everything that God does is listed in the Bible (John 21:25, "and there are also many other things which Jesus did, which if they were written in detail, I suppose that even the world itself would not contain the books that would be written"). But what God does will not go against His Bible, because He is not a liar (Titus 1:2, "in the hope of eternal life, which God who cannot lie, promised long ages ago"). Feeling the presence of the Spirit is a good reason to receive the laying on of hands many times, because in His presence there is great joy (Psalms 16:11, "you (God) will make known to me the path of life; in your presence is fullness of joy; in your right hand there are pleasures forever"). So be filled with the Holy Spirit over and over (Ephesians 5:18). Imagine yourself as a cup overflowing with God and touching others with His love (Psalms 23:5). It is so much fun!

And finally the third outcome of the laying on hands: physical healing. Healing is in the covenant we have with Christ. Isaiah 53 is chapter prophesying about Jesus. Verses four and five state,

> "surely our griefs (or sickness) He Himself bore, and our sorrows He carried; yet we ourselves He carried; yet we ourselves esteemed Him stricken, smitten of God, and afflicted but He was pierced (or wounded) for our transgressions, He was crushed for our transgressions, He was crushed for our iniquities; the chastening for our well-being fell upon Him, and by His scourging we are healed."

The book of Matthew gives insight to Isaiah when it says in Matthew 8:16–17, "When evening came, they brought to Him (Jesus) many who were demon-possessed; and He cast out the spirits with a word, and healed all who were ill. This was to fulfill what was spoken through the Isaiah the prophet: 'He Himself took our infirmities and carried away our diseases.'" God did this because He is a good father. Sin and sickness came into the world because Adam and Eve gave authority to the devil. Now the devil oppresses people (Luke 13:11–16). But Jesus came to destroy the works of the devil (1 John 3:8). This was accomplished through the death and resurrection of

Christ. That is why the Bible states in Him we have been healed (1 Peter 2:24). Yet, one of the ways it is enforced or enacted is by the "laying on of hands."

Physical healing has two expressions. These two are called healings and miracles. The Bible speaks about the gift of working miracles in 1 Corinthians 12:29. A miracle is an instantaneous physical healing, while a healing is progressive. I do not know why there are some instantaneous miracles and some progressive healings. Jesus prayed for someone twice, and some others were healed as they went (Mark 8:25, Luke 17:14). As you lay hands on people, you will see miracles and healings. Both are good.

I would be remiss to not tell you that God cannot be put into a box. He does all of these things mentioned, even without the laying on of hands. God is creative and powerful, and you will see Him do incredible wonders, yet I doubt the laying on hands will ever stop.

A man named John Wimber designed a simple five-step prayer model to help people pray for the sick. You can learn more about this in Randy Clark's *Healing School Manual*, but I want to provide you with the basics of it. You do not have to be a super spiritual Christian to pray for people to be healed. You do not have to get all the words right. This model may help you as it has helped thousands of other people. Do it at a grocery store; it is exciting! I have seen scores of people healed and so can you!

Five-Step Prayer Model:

Step 1: The Interview: Hi my name is____. What is wrong?

Step 2: Diagnosis: Do you know when this problem began? What was going on in your life during that time? May I pray for you? (Ask if you can touch them. If not, that is okay).

Step 3: Prayer Selection: Choose prayer style. Jesus often spoke directly to a problem and commanded it to leave, and others in Scripture did the same. This could look like you telling pain to leave someone's body. You may also ask God to come and heal.

> Example: Thank you, Father. Pain in knee, I command you to leave in the name of Jesus. Amen.

Step 4: Prayer Ministry: This is where you actually pray. When praying in a public place, use normal talking volume and voice and don't close your eyes.

Step 5: Post-Prayer Suggestions: Ask them to attempt something they could not do or to check for pain. Ask them to check if there is any difference. If so, then ask what how much it improved. If needed, ask if you can pray for them again. Encourage their walk with the Lord. (Ex: Do you consider yourself a follower of Jesus?) If they are not healed thank them for allowing you to pray for them. Always praise God!

Read John chapter 9. Still yourself and place yourself in John 9:1–11. Come to Jesus and ask Him one of these questions:

1. How can I grow in love and step out to pray for people?

2. How important is praying for other people?

Here is a place for you to write down any questions you have that came up while reading this lesson. Take your questions to a person of spiritual maturity that you trust.

_____

_____

_____

Question: Why will God continue to use "laying on of hands?"

_____

_____

_____

DAY 10:
WITNESSING

It still brings up emotions when I think of it today. I was watching a popular television show in which a rich man was in a hut with a dying family in Africa. He was visiting to help raise support to help the poor and sick. While in that hut, he was overwhelmed with how different his world was compared to the hut he was standing in. It broke his heart because he knew there was a better life. He kept saying, "this should not be."

This is one of the most powerful pictures I know to describe witnessing. Acts 1:8 states that we will be the witnesses of Jesus when we have received the Holy Spirit. In the kingdom of God, there is no pain, poverty, sadness, or demonic oppression. It is the desire of Jesus that it "be on earth as it is in heaven" (Matthew 6:10). This change on earth happens through His witnesses, through you and me. Your heart will break the more you realize how amazing the kingdom of God is and how awful it is to be in the kingdom of darkness.

The Bible states that everyone is a minister! We all have the ministry of reconciliation (2 Corinthians 5:18). This is bringing people to God to get right with Him, to become a follower of Christ. How can you do this? First, it is good to have established a couple of truths in your heart. One is that God wants everyone to be right with Him (2 Peter 3:9), and the second is that it is God's job to bring people to Christ (John 6:44). With these truth in place we also need to know that while God does want everyone in right relationship with Him and that He is the only one that can draw people to Himself, He wants to work with us. 1 Corinthians 3:9 states we are co-laborers or "fellow workers" with Christ. This means that God wants you to partner with Him in revealing His love and His kingdom to people around you.

So what do you do? You simply become a witness. Show people and tell people about the reality of Jesus by demonstrating God's love through prayer and good deeds. People tend to more readily believe in Jesus after they have experienced a miracle or seen real love in action through kindness. You can tell them by explaining to them that what they just experienced was God. Then ask them if they want to be a follower of Christ. If they say yes, pray with them to ask Jesus to be the Lord of their life (Romans 10:9, "that if you confess with your mouth Jesus as Lord, and believe in your heart that God raised Him from the dead, you will be saved"). Then if possible, invite them to church with you or recommend them to a local church.

Remember that becoming a follower of Jesus is as simple as a prayer and yet more than a prayer. God desires disciples, or followers (Matthew 28:19, "make disciples of all the nations"). He is not looking for people to say a prayer and then leave Him behind. Jesus longs for people that will learn about His kingdom and get to know Him. This person is a follower of Christ. You cannot earn your way to God. Jesus did all the work on the cross to provide the way to be right with Him *except* to make people believe. If someone is willing to give all of their life to God through Jesus, then they can be His follower. Jesus is looking for people that will give themselves away to Him (submit their lives to Him as Lord), develop a relationship with Him (be a daily follower), and to enter into His design and destiny for their lives— for Him to make them into something (look up Matthew 4:19 and 16:24).

It is good to let them know that Jesus died because of how valuable they are to Him. God is crazy in love with them, has a plan for their lives, and wants to restore them to their original values. Jesus did not simply die because of sin. He died because they were not created to be sinners, and He wants to restore them to how He designed them to be! As you learn more about what life is like in the kingdom of heaven you will look around and feel the heart of God rise up in you declaring, "this should not be!" People were not created to be selfish, hurting, depressed, hateful, lustful, sick, or stressed out. Friends, this should not be and you can do something about it!

I want to encourage you to invite your friends to church. Pray for the sick and hurting people. Live the real life of a follower of Christ in front of people. It is okay to talk about God without "preaching" to them. Get involved in the lives of people around you as Jesus was when He was called "a friend of sinners"

(Matthew 11:19). Help the poor and hurting in your community. Simply love people where they are and do not hide that you serve a wonderful God. Answer any questions they ask and ask people if they want to become a follower of Jesus Christ. God will help you! You do not have to have all the answers. He sees all the hurting people and longs for them to come to Him (Matthew 11:28, 2 Peter 3:9).

Read John chapter 10. Still yourself and place yourself in John 10:40–42. Come to Jesus and ask Him one of these questions:

    1. What are some things that "should not be?"

    2. Who in my life can I reach out to?

Here is a place for you to write down any questions you have that came up while reading this lesson. Take your questions to a person of spiritual maturity that you trust.

_____

_____

_____

Question: How can you include God in everyday relationships?

_____

_____

_____

# DAY 11:
WHO YOU ARE

There are two fundamental questions that everyone must answer: "Is there a God?" and "Who am I?" The answers to these questions set the context for how every person interacts in their world. If you believe that God does not exist, then you have no hope in life. If you believe that you are worthless, then you will treat yourself that way and expect others to do the same.

Some people have picked up on how important the answer is to the second question. That is why there are so many "positive thinking" books. The only problem with them is that they have no secure foundation. In other words, you may say that you are great. But why? How can you really know that you are great? The fact is you need your Creator to tell you your value.

Only the one that made you can accurately define your worth. This is the reason that poor parenting hurts people so much. We naturally look to those who brought us into this world to give us our value. Unfortunately, many parents do not ascribe the proper value to their children. So no matter how hard they work at it, many people can never really get beyond the rejection that came from Mom and Dad. We inaccurately learned our identity from them.

If you believe in God, then you can go beyond your parents to gain your identity. Even if you have great parents, their words can only go so far. Everyone needs to know their value from their Creator. Knowing who you are to God establishes something in your heart that no amount of a human's positive self talk can provide.

We instinctively know by God that helping other people is good. Yet, you cannot truly serve others without knowing your own value. Why? Because you will always be seeking someone's approval, which then turns your service into selfishness. You need them to value your sacrifice or give some type of thanks for the help. If you are confident in who you are, then you can serve others whether or not they recognize you.

Then, your service is not about you but about love. God wants to free you from you! When you receive your value from God, you are free from needing validation from others and free from selfishness.

Jesus said it this way, "love your neighbor as yourself" (Matthew 19:19). If the truth were told, many people would hate their neighbors if they loved them like they love themselves. Loving yourself is important, and it only comes from knowing who you are to God.

So what does your Creator think about you? What is your identity and value to God? Your value and your identity can both be known through the death and resurrection of Jesus.

The value of a house is set by what it can sell for. Location, location, location! If you built a million-dollar house in a trailer park, you would never be able to sell it for a million dollars. So in a sense, it is not really worth a million dollars. Likewise, if you put a shack on beachfront property in California, you could get a lot of money for it. Do you realize how much was paid for you? The most valuable price possible was paid for your life! Jesus died for you. So how valuable does that make you? The Bible even tells us that God loves us as much as He loves Jesus (John

17:23)! I would not believe it unless it was in the Bible, but since it is, I do. The primary basis you can always go to in your heart to know that God loves you is that Jesus died for you. No matter how you feel or how your day is going, the proof of God's love is found in the death and resurrection of Christ Jesus.

The death and resurrection of Jesus did not just save us from an eternal punishment in hell. It was also the means to become a child of God (John 1:12). That is right! You are royalty from heaven's perspective. Hard to believe? Look up Galatians 4:7 and 1 Peter 2:9. You are not a mistake! God picked the time and place for you to live (Acts 17:26). You are God's dream come true!

The more you know and believe the fact of who you are in Christ, the more you can truly love and serve others. So here's how it works. A powerful way of knowing who you are is found in hearing from God. You need to hear from God through the Bible. You also need to hear from God through two-way journaling. You may also need to hear from God in your own voice by quoting His promises aloud.

Take your Bible and look up all the verses about being "in Christ." You can go to www.crosswalk.

com and utilize the "Bible Study Tools" option. If you use that option you can type in "in Christ" and set the "Filter Results" to the "Pauline Epistles" for a good start. You can also go so blueletter-bible.org for help. Journal about God's thoughts about you and say out loud to yourself what God has said. It may seem like a strange exercise, but it is very powerful to look in the mirror at yourself and confess God's love in personal language like, "You are loved by your heavenly Father!"

Perhaps you are asking yourself how this is different than positive self-talk. The difference is that you are telling yourself who God has said you are. His words carry a lot more weight than simple positive talk and change you from the inside out. Self-talk is good when it is founded on His Words! It will take time, and it may feel awkward at first, but it is worth it.

Proverbs 23:7 says, "As he thinks within Himself, so he is." Do you see how big this is? You do not perceive life as it is. You view life as you see yourself. If you think no one wants you around, then you will interpret everyone's actions to confirm what you believe! But if you know in your heart that you are loved, then you will be free to love others with no strings attached. It will give you confidence to pray for people as royalty and not as a beggar. Most importantly, you can approach God as His beloved child and not as a slave. This lesson is just the tip of the iceberg of how important identity is. As you mature, you will be amazed at how important it is to know who you are to God. Have fun discovering your identity in Christ!

Read John chapter 11. Still yourself and place yourself in John 11:23–44. Come to Jesus and ask Him one of these questions:

> 1. What is my value to you?
>
> 2. What can I confess daily about your love for me?

Here is a place for you to write down any questions you have that came up while reading this lesson. Take your questions to a person of spiritual maturity that you trust.

....

....

....

Question: How do your self-image and God's image of you compare?

....

....

....

DAY 12: HISTORY

It is always the desire of a good father for his children to do better than he did. You will never find a good father jealous at the success of his child. The same is true with God. This desire is expressed in the words of Christ when He said, "he who believes in Me, the works that I do, he will do also; and greater…" (John 14:12).

This is a beautiful picture of building upon what Christ has done and taking it further. Only one can die for the sins of the world, but Jesus wants us to see more miracles happen in our lives than He did in His life. God is creative and wants to do things that have never been done before. He literally wants you to do greater works than Jesus did. Jesus will not be jealous. You will make Him extremely happy by building on what He started.

However, it is nearly impossible to build up when we do not know what was built before us. How can you build the second story on a building if the first floor gets torn down every time you start? That is how many people approach Church history. We do not know what has happened, so we cannot learn from their mistakes, and we cannot build upon their successes.

Why are there so many denominations? What miracles did our forefathers see? What lessons were they teaching about Christ? We do not need to reinvent the wheel every generation! You have a great potential to skyrocket in your spiritual maturity if you learn from others.

Others have strived and gained new ground in the Spirit. We can honor them and honor God by learning from them and pressing on toward more. Those who have died before us are watching (Hebrews 12:1). I believe that they want to see what we do with the spiritual ground that they laid. Do not start from scratch! Do not start over what someone else has already done. Learn Church history and advance beyond what anyone has done before.

Do greater works than Jesus did! This is your calling and destiny.

Read John chapter 12. Still yourself and place yourself in John 12:27–33. Come to Jesus and ask Him one of these questions:

1. What area of church history should I start with?

2. How do I do greater works than you, Jesus?

Here is a place for you to write down any questions you have that came up while reading this lesson. Take your questions to a person of spiritual maturity that you trust.

Question: How important do you think history is to God?

DAY 13:
THE HEART

Someone once said that life begins with a spanking and only gets worse from there. While I do not agree with life getting worse, I do agree that life has its painful moments. Just like you, I have experienced pain.

My mother married five men. My dad married three women and also died of cancer. I had a very abusive step dad, one that was a drunk, and one that seemed to think he was right no matter how obvious it was that he was wrong. I also grew up in poverty. Our trailer was run down and filled with roaches. I lived most of my childhood in survival mode. We were just trying to make it to the next day. No family traditions, no family game night, just surviving. Unfortunately, my childhood is not unlike many.

Each of the people in my life has their own story. They were dealing with their own issues. Thankfully, my mom has received what she needed to be secure in God. I am not sure about the others. However, even though I know they were acting out of their own insecurities, it does not change the fact that a person cannot go through that type of lifestyle without having issues. Truth be told, everyone has their own issues they deal with, even if their life has been good.

I tell you some of my story not to compete with your story. I am sure I would "lose" to many people. It is only told here as a platform for dealing with the truth. Every person on this planet has been hurt at some time. Many have their personalities and their approach to life shaped by these wounds in their heart.

This lesson is not designed to bring healing in all of your life pains and confusions. It is here to equip you with the truth. If you are breathing air, you have been hurt by someone. Thankfully, you do not have to remain shaped and controlled by these hurts. Jesus said, "Come to me all you who are weary and heavy laden and I will give you rest" (Matthew

11:28). You can come to Him and receive refreshment for your soul and freedom from your pain. Jesus did not cause the bad evil to happen, but He can heal you if you let him.

If you are interested in not being controlled by emotional pain, then you are already on your way to being healed. What you need to do is to connect with some people that can help you. Being vulnerable may not be easy but it will be worth it.

God loves to work through people in bringing healing to the heart because it draws us closer together. The Bible tells us to confess our faults to each other so that we can be healed (James 5:16). Within a group of people that you can feel safe to reveal your inner pain to comes a deep and lasting healing. The thing to remember is that life is a journey, and it can take time to receive the freedom we seek.

You will find that most emotional healing comes through an internal realization of what Christ has done for you, thinks of you, through repentance (explained tomorrow) and forgiveness. As you embrace what Christ has done for you and your identity in Christ you will find freedom in many areas. Even though this may seem simple, it cannot be done simply through head knowledge. In other words, it sort of has to "dawn on you."

I know what it is like to be emotionally hurt. Fortunately, I also know what it is like to be healed. You do not have to go through life with emotional baggage. There is freedom. Perhaps you think that you do not have anything you need to be healed from. This is a dangerous place to be in. The Bible states that there is a way that seems right in us, but the end leads only to death (Proverbs 14:12). If you cannot accept that there is a possibility that you are living out of a hurting heart, then you will hurt people without even knowing it. You may even have heard people say, "hurt people hurt people."

So how can you know if you are hurting emotionally? Jesus said that a good tree produces good fruit and likewise a bad tree, bad fruit (Matthew 7:17). This is typically called "fruit to root." When there are attitudes and actions that don't match what the Bible says that you are in Christ then you are looking at some "bad fruit." For example as you notice something like rage in your life, know that the rage itself is not the real issue. There is a root in your heart that feeds that rage. If you only attempt to conquer the fruit (rage, for example), you will not have real victory. Real freedom can only come through a change in heart and mind.

Most of the time you will find the root issue to be self-centeredness, insecurities, and a lack of love. Jesus is the answer! Bring your root issue to Him in prayer. Worship Him for the truth of who you are in Christ and watch as your root issue dissolves. Whether you feel loved or not you are loved. The death and resurrection of Christ is the proof. Nothing you go through or feel can take that away. Fix your heart on what the Bible says. The truth is you were not created to be bitter or selfish and that you are incredibly loved by God. While hurt people hurt people, loved people love people and healed people heal people. Seek out the help of your leadership for any counseling you need and help others with the help God gives you.

Read John chapter 13. Still yourself and place yourself in John 13:3–11. After Jesus washes your feet, ask Him one of these questions:

1. What "fruit" in my life is from hurt?

2. What do you have to say about that hurt?

Here is a place for you to write down any questions you have that came up while reading this lesson. Take your questions to a person of spiritual maturity that you trust.

_____

_____

_____

Question: How can you take steps to achieving emotional healing?

_____

_____

_____

# DAY 14:
REPENTANCE

Repentance is a Bible word that means *to change your mind about something*. In everyday life, I repent when I learn something new. Let me illustrate with a little story.

On a packed flight, people found themselves very annoyed with a man. He would not control his two children, who were crying, screaming, and running up and down the aisle. At last, a stewardess asked him to do something with his children. He turned to her with tears in his eyes, apologized, and said, "We are just leaving the funeral of their mother and my wife." Suddenly the children were not annoying anymore! Now the children were surrounded by people that wanted to bounce them on their knees and play with them. In this story, the people repented, or changed their mind, about the children and the father when they learned the circumstances.

In relation to God, we repent when we see things from God's perspective. Repentance enables us to see or to have the truths of God's kingdom "dawn on us." Jesus said it this way, "repent, for the Kingdom of heaven is at hand" (Matthew 3:2). When we repent, we are able to see that Jesus is alive, that sinning is not beneficial, and that God has provided us with access to His kingdom (His way of doing things, His provision, His power, and His angels).

So how do you repent? Ask for it. It is a gift (2 Timothy 2:25). It is connected with hearing from God and acting on it. Acting on it is proof of repentance or "the fruit of repentance" (Luke 3:8). After God has shown you a truth through the Bible, two-way journaling, a preacher, reading a book, or another way, and you believe it, then you have just repented! When someone accepts that Jesus is the only way to be right with God, they have repented. You will repent many times about thinking incorrectly or about sinning against God. When your belief has turned into action, then you have completed the circle of repentance with providing fruit. And let me tell you, friend, God loves to see fruit in your life (John 15:2–4).

Since repentance is changing *your* mind about something, it is not enough for someone else to believe for you. You cannot be right with God because someone in your family is right with God. Each person must repent for themselves (Acts 2:38).

Please do not make the mistake of thinking that you have fully grasped a spiritual truth just because you read it or heard it once. When it seems like God has told you the truth you read or heard, then you have taken a big step toward real repentance. You make it your own through prayer, studying the Bible, two-way journaling, talking with others about it, and doing it. If you tried it out and it did not seem to work, but you can see it in the Bible, then keep doing it and keep praying. God rewards those who diligently seek Him (Hebrews 11:6). Repenting is a beautiful process that leads us to see that God's ways are always good, even if they are different from what we knew before (Isaiah 55:8–9).

Read John chapter 14. Still yourself and place yourself in John 14:1–6. Come to Jesus and ask Him one of these questions:

1. What spiritual truth do I know but still need to believe?

2. How important is repentance?

Here is a place for you to write down any questions you have that came up while reading this lesson. Take your questions to a person of spiritual maturity that you trust.

_____

_____

_____

Question: How does repentance relate to our actions?

_____

_____

_____

DAY 15:
HOLINESS

What does a holy God look like to you? If you are like many people, a holy God looks like an old man with a long beard that sits on a throne and never smiles or has any fun. Many people believe that God is always angry and ready to destroy the world because He is holy, which to them means angry and untouchable. Wow! Who would want to serve a god like that?

Interestingly enough, the Bible gives us a different picture of God (and of Jesus). In a little book in the Bible called Zephaniah, we are told that God rejoices over His people with shouts of joy (3:17B). The word translated into *rejoice* literally means *to spin round wildly under the influence of any violent emotion* (the emotion in this verse being joy). Check out Strong's Concordance # 1523 for the *guwl*. How about that as a picture of a holy God?

Have you seen many pictures depicting Jesus with a smile? I haven't. Why not? People assume that he was angry all the time for two reasons. One is that the Bible does not specifically state that Jesus smiled. The other is that people assume that because he is holy, he has to be angry most of the time. Yet, Hebrews 1:9 states that Jesus was anointed with the oil of gladness (or joy) above all His companions. This implies that Jesus has more gladness than anyone you have ever met! Jesus walked the earth a happy guy!

What does all this have to do with holiness? Well, too many people seem to think that following God takes the joy out of life. They think following Christ means that you look like you have been sucking on a lemon. This is the picture people have about living a holy life. Again, who would want to serve a god like that?

According to a Webster's Collegiate Dictionary, *holiness* means *exalted or worthy of complete devotion as one perfect in goodness and righteousness.* Holiness is about complete devotion. It is first and foremost a matter of the heart. I heard someone say that holiness is not about saying no to something; it is about saying yes to Someone! As you develop a relationship with God, holiness, known as the "fruit of the Spirit" will come naturally (Galatians 5:22–24).

Here is an example of saying yes to someone. My wife does things for me that someone else might see and think they would never do. Yet, my wife does not think about it as a sacrifice. She is just loving me in a way that is meaningful for me. That is holiness in a nutshell, loving God in a way that is meaningful to Him! God finds holiness beautiful (Psalm 29:2, New King James Version).

Is it wrong for a married couple to expect each other to be faithful? Not at all! Why? Because they are married and have committed their lives to each other specifically. The Bible tells us that when you gave your life to Christ, you came into a spiritual relationship with God that is as strong, and even stronger, than marriage (Ephesians 5:22–27, 32). So is it wrong for God to expect you to live completely devoted to Him? Absolutely not.

You will grow in your knowledge of what pleases and displeases God over time. The best place to learn this is from the Bible. I am not going to provide you a list of do's and don'ts, because holiness is action that comes from the heart and not the other way around. In fact, God hates it when our actions are right and our hearts are wrong (Isaiah 29:13). The basic premise of holiness is that God longs for us to love Him and love others. It is that simple.

You may have heard the word *sin*. It is an English translation of a few different words in the Bible. To sin is basically doing something wrong. As simple as that concept sounds, sin is a big deal. Jesus died to restore us to His original plan because something huge was in the way—sin. Sin separated us from God (Colossians 1:21–22).

Thankfully, Jesus died to reconcile the whole world to God (1 John 2:2). Jesus lived a completely holy life and became sin on the cross in order to restore you to Himself (2 Corinthians 5:21). After you have accepted Him as your Lord, you can live a life that promotes deeper intimacy with God. Holiness does not equal intimacy with God, just as fidelity in marriage does not equal intimacy, but it is an important aspect of real intimacy.

At this point, I need to let you in on a secret. It is impossible for you to live a holy life on your own. The Bible even tells us that it really is impossible to do anything without God (John 15:5). In holiness, God calls us to perfection. He says to be holy as He is holy (1 Peter 1:16).

The entire Christian life is impossible without God! Thankfully, you are not on your own! Jesus states that when He sets you free from sin, then you are truly free (John 8:36). Romans 6:1–14 confirms the freedom we gain from the death and resurrection of Christ.

If you try to live holy on your own, you will either live in frustration or you will live with pride as you look down on others who could not just determine to live holy like you did. Frustration will come from failure; pride will come from self-willed success. Pride is a sin, and God resists the proud (1 Peter 5:5). The best way to walk in holiness is to ask for God's help. He wants to help keep you from evil (Matthew 6:13). The help he gives is grace, *unmerited favor and divine enablement.*

Our spirits are freed from sin through the cross, but our minds and emotions go through a process.

The more freedom you get in God's love, the more freedom you will have from sinful habits. This is an important aspect of emotional healing. Most sins are from a desire to meet an emotional need that God wants to meet. Finally, allow me to encourage you never to believe any idea about holiness that state you have to sin. Never believe any idea that implies the power of the devil is more powerful than God's ability to set you free. If you do sin, come to God and ask Him to forgive you (1 John 1:9–2:2). Always run to God. He will accept you and help you.

You were not created to sin. The Bible makes it clear that you were created in God's image and likeness (Genesis 1:26–27). Now, I understand that we have all sinned. We have all done things that are not good. Thankfully, as I have shown, this is not the end of the story. Not only does God provide forgiveness but also provides the availability for you to live in His nature, which is pure and holy (2 Peter 1:4). I personally have seen incredible personal freedom, as I simply tell God that I accept His nature and thank Him for allowing me to participate in His divine nature.

Read John chapter 15. Still yourself and place yourself in John 15:1–11. Come to Jesus and ask Him one
of these questions:

1. What can I say yes to that pleases you?

2. What can I say no to that would not please
you?

Here is a place for you to write down any questions you have that came up while reading this lesson. Take your questions to a person of spiritual maturity that you trust.

_____

_____

_____

Question: How do you learn what standard to live by?

_____

_____

_____

# DAY 16: JUDGMENT

There is an end to life as we know it. Hebrews 6:1–2 states some basic things to know, two of which are that God will resurrect all the bodies of those that have died and that there is an eternal judgment. You must know that everyone will stand before God to face judgment, and no one will enter heaven that does not want to be there.

The Bible makes it clear that those in Christ have little to be concerned about. Romans 8:1 states "there is no condemnation to those that are in Christ." Jesus took on Himself the punishment we deserved. So we stand innocent in judgment. However, those who have rejected Christ will face eternity in hell. This is called the second death (Revelation 20:14). The first is physical, and the second is separation from the presence of God forever (2 Thessalonians 1:9).

What followers of Christ have to personally be aware of is whether they live from a pure conscience. If you have access to a *Strong's Concordance* or an online concordance, look up *conscience* and you will quickly see that a pure conscience is very important to God. All that you do in this life will face a judgment called *being tested by fire* (1 Corinthians 3:13, "each man's work will become evident; for the day will show it because it is to be revealed with fire, and the fire itself will test the quality of each man's work"). This is where God exposes what we have done with pure motives in obedience to Him and what we have not done.

For this reason, Philippians 2:12 tells us to work out our salvation with "fear and trembling." Standing before the One who loves you more passionately than anyone in the world and showing Him all the times that something was not done out of love is not going to be a fun event. Live from a pure conscience. It will bring your heavenly Father great joy forever and will shape your actions.

Living from a pure conscience will also set you up for rewards. In Revelation 22:12 Jesus states, "Behold, I am coming quickly, and My reward is with Me, to render to every man what he has done." It is the desire of God to give us rewards. Even if you give a cup of cold water to someone in His name that you would be rewarded (Matthew 10:42). God longs to pour out rewards on His followers that will last for all eternity.

Imagine the type of rewards that the creator of all things can give! Some people think it is bad to think about getting rewarded. I think it is good, since He did it (Hebrews 12:2). If it is okay for Jesus to do something for the reward, then it is okay for His followers. Sometimes holding on to the promise of rewards will help people make it through a difficult time. It helped Jesus.

You know living with a pure conscience is important. With that established, let your heart burn for those that are not right with God. It is they who need your prayers and God's love through your life. They are facing a resurrection after physical death only to face a second death. This second death for them will be worse than I can possibly describe. There is a resurrection of the dead, and there is an eternal judgment. You can set yourself up for rewards by walking with God with a pure conscience and help others by loving them with God's love. It is His goodness, which can come through you, that leads people to repentance (Romans 2:4B, "the kindness of God leads you to repentance").

Read John chapter 16. Still yourself and place yourself in John 16:1–15. Come to Jesus and ask Him one of these questions:

> 1. Is there an area where I feel condemnation? How do you see me in that area?
>
> 2. How can I display Your goodness today?

Here is a place for you to write down any questions you have that came up while reading this lesson. Take your questions to a person of spiritual maturity that you trust.

_____

_____

_____

Question: Knowing that Christ took upon Himself your judgment, what does that make you want to do?

_____

_____

_____

DAY 17:
JESUS'S RETURN

Jesus said, "In My Father's house are many dwelling places; if it were not so, I would have told you; for I go to prepare a place for you, I will come again and receive you to Myself, that where I am, there you may be also" (John 14:2–3).

God cannot lie (Titus 1:2). His word states Jesus will return and that all eyes will see Him on that day (Revelation 1:7). Jesus told us that it would be a long time before he came back (Luke 20:9). So far, it has been about 2,000 years. Yet, we know He could come back at any moment (Matthew 24:42).

There are many, many beliefs about what the return of Christ will look like and what could be signs foreshadowing that He is about to return. This simple book is not designed to explore all of these

Benjamin and Micah Joy Williams

ideas, so I recommend finding out what your church believes and studying on your own as well.

Maybe you are thinking to yourself that understanding the return of Jesus Christ is not that important. After all, He said that He will come back, and I believe Him. So, what does that have to do with my everyday life anyway? Everything!

If you believe, like some Christians do, that Jesus will return to an earth in which His Church (every believer) is living a defeated or self-absorbed life, then you will shape your life to fit that expectation. In other words, if you believe that the purpose of the return of Christ is to rescue the Church from defeat, then you will think that living a defeated lifestyle is somehow normal and that you are actually helping to cause Jesus to want to come back. Understand?

You may not realize it, but you are entering into a "culture." This is a Christian culture that has ideas, values, and expectations. Though you may not know anything about the return of Jesus, you can be influenced by the culture you happen to be in and what that culture believes.

Here is one more example.

When I met my wife's family, I quickly learned something. Their sense of humor included something mine did not. It included quoting movie lines. I missed many jokes that everyone else was laughing at because I had no idea that it was a joke. I had entered into a culture that included humor using movie lines.

So, what do you think I did? I watched movies. I wanted to fit in, to get the jokes, and maybe even to tell a few. While the jury is still out as to whether I have ever told a joke that was beyond "corny" or not, I have tried. You see, there was a history that shaped a culture that I entered into, which in turn affected how I lived.

Every church has a history when it comes to what they believe concerning the return of Jesus. This idea has directly or indirectly shaped how that church approaches life. And when someone comes into that church, they are changed by that culture, even if they do not know anything about what the church believes.

Understanding that Jesus is returning and what the Church will look like when He returns is vitally important. In Ephesians 5, we catch a glimpse of what the Church will look like when He returns.

Ephesians 5:27 states, "that He (Jesus) might present to Himself the Church in all her glory, having no spot or wrinkle or any such thing; but that she would be holy and blameless" (parenthesis added). Simply said, Jesus is returning for a Church that is glorious and beautiful.

When I got married, I would have been very surprised if my bride had shown up on our wedding day wearing pajamas. I was expecting her to wear her wedding gown, and to have done all the things brides do to prepare for that day. Was it wrong for me to expect this? Of course not.

The Bible compares the Church to a bride in Ephesians 5:25–32. It is the spiritual Bride of Christ. Is it wrong for Jesus to want His Bride to be glorious and beautiful? Of course not. And this is exactly what He expects. The Church Jesus is coming back for is not one that is beat up by the devil, living in sin, and barely making it in life. Jesus is coming back for a victorious Church that is shining with all His glory and walking above reproach (Ephesians 5:27).

What does it look like to be a glorious Church? It is a Church that is living a life of faith (Luke 18:8). A glorious Church is doing the works that Christ did (John 14:12). It is living a life of genuine concern for people (Matthew 25:31–46). The glorious Church is also a Church that is walking in intimacy with Jesus (John 17:3; the word "know" here means *an intimate knowing*).

No matter what you discover about what your church believes concerning the return of Jesus Christ, know two things: Know that Jesus Christ is returning. He is not still a little baby in a manger. Jesus is the King of kings and Lord of lords (Revelation 19:11–16)! And know what the Church (including you) is going to look like at His appearing. Your destiny is to be a part of this glorious Church. Allow that truth to shape how you live and what you expect!

Read John chapter 17. Still yourself and place your-self in John 17:22–25. Come to Jesus and ask Him one of these questions:

1. How can I get ready for your return?

2. How do I help the Church become the glo-rious Bride?

Here is a place for you to write down any questions you have that came up while reading this lesson. Take your questions to a person of spiritual maturity that you trust.

_____

_____

_____

Question: What do you currently believe about the return of Christ?

_____

_____

_____

# DAY 18:
SACRAMENTS

"Sacraments" is a fancy term not used in the Bible. It means certain things that are to be regularly practiced and considered sacred. They are holy traditions that were established by Jesus Christ. Most churches hold to two sacraments. One is water baptism, and the other is Holy Communion.

Each church tradition or denomination has a little different understanding about these two sacraments, but most believe them to be very important. I want to look at them briefly, but you should research what your church believes and participate if you can.

The Bible records that the twelve disciples of Jesus baptized people (John 4:2). It also records Jesus saying, "Go therefore and make disciples of all nations, baptizing them in the name of the Father and the Son and the Holy Spirit" (Matthew 28:19). Jesus believed in water baptism.

Some churches sprinkle water, and others immerse people in water. Some churches have special pitchers to pour the water, while others do not. Some churches have a special place for baptizing inside the church building called a baptismal, while others immerse people in a river or a swimming pool. What is important is to know what your church believes and why your church holds that belief. I also recommend reading Romans 6:1–11 prayerfully to gain insight to the power that can be released through a faith-filled baptism.

Another sacrament instituted by Christ is Communion. First Corinthians 11:23–26 is a commonly used passage for this sacrament. It was started by Christ as a reminder of what He went through so that you and I could be right with God. It shows us that being forgiven of sin was not cheap. It cost Jesus His life. Communion reminds us of how important God thinks His relationship is with us. This sacrament established your value for all time. It is where we can come and celebrate the victory He had over sin, death, and the grave! Communion is so much more than I could write here.

This sacrament is so beautiful and intimate. Many people feel closer to God during Communion than at any other time. Perhaps that is one reason it is called, "Communion." You see, all the effects of sin were placed on Jesus. "He Who knew no sin became sin for us" (2 Corinthians 5:21). Communion is a connecting point to what Jesus's death and resurrection accomplished. That is why many people receive physical healing while taking Communion.

Communion is another area about which people believe a little differently. It would be good for you to find out what your church believes and practices with Communion. Participating in Communion and remembering what Christ has done for you will enrich your relationship with Christ.

Read chapter 18. Still yourself and place yourself in John 18:1. Come to Jesus in the garden and ask Him one of these questions:

1. How important is water baptism?
2. How do you see Holy Communion?

Here is a place for you to write down any questions you have that came up while reading this lesson. Take your questions to a person of spiritual maturity that you trust.

_____

_____

_____

Question: What does your church believe about the sacraments?

_____

_____

_____

DAY 19: SPIRITUAL LAW

What goes up must come down. Gravity. This is called a law of nature. Natural laws work for anyone. If you are the nicest person on the earth, they will work for you. If you happen to be the worst person on the face of the planet, they would still work for you. Just as there are natural laws, there are spiritual laws.

The same is true for spiritual laws. God causes the sun to shine and the rain to fall on the righteous and the unrighteous (Matthew 5:45). It is in God's heart to provide blessings even to those who do not know Him. The blessings in Christ far outweigh the blessings outside of a relationship with Jesus but He loves on all humanity. He cannot help Himself. "God is love" (1 John 4:8).

These spiritual laws can be seen in the Bible as things that are not directly related to any commandment and work for anyone. As a follower of Christ, these laws are extremely powerful. I want to look at a few of them with you. There are more, but here are some with which to start. They are sowing and reaping, the power of agreement, and the power given to the tongue.

Sowing and reaping is a simple but powerful spiritual law. It can easily be seen in nature. When a farmer sows corn, the farmer expects to reap corn. If you sow studying for a test, you are more likely reap a passing score. If a couple sows counseling into marriage, they will reap the benefits of a better marriage. The Bible says it this way, "Do not be deceived, God is not mocked; for whatever a man sows, this he will also reap" (Galatians 6:7). This is a simple law that touches all of life and operates in the lives of followers of Christ and unbelievers. I will show you in another way.

As I read some financial books from the perspective of unbelievers, I was shocked to find the spiritual law of sowing and reaping in their materials. I read in several books where the authors said that they did not know why, but they found that if they gave money away, more money would come to them. In other words, when they sowed money like a seed, they would reap more money like a harvest. This was not from a Christian perspective, but it was truly a spiritual law in action. Second Corinthians 9:6 states about giving money, "Now this I say, he who sows sparingly will also reap sparingly, and he who sows bountifully will also reap bountifully."

I do not know about you, but I find it amazing that this works for anyone. Yet in a Christian's life, it works better and has deeper meaning than for an unbeliever. An aspect of this law is giving the tithe (a tenth of your earnings) to your church. This began in Genesis 4:3–4, and Jesus commanded it in Luke 11:42. When you give your tithe and offerings above your tithe, you are sowing into God's kingdom and showing God that you trust Him to take care of you. God promises that as you sow, you will reap His provision every time (Philippians 4:17–19). God even challenges you to test Him in tithes and offerings to see if He will bless you greatly (Malachi 3:8–12). So I challenge you to give to your local church. They are not after your money. They are after you being taken care of by God.

Another powerful spiritual law is the power of agreement. The Bible states that when some unbelievers were in agreement on building a tower into heaven, "nothing which they purpose to do will be impossible for them" (Genesis 11:6). God was the only power strong enough to stop them, because they were in agreement. When a person comes to Christ, agreement takes on even more power than this. Jesus said that if two or more people would agree about anything in His Name, it would happen (Matthew 18:19). This is why praying with people and being together with believers is so important. If applied, the potential for impacting the world is unparalleled.

Finally, there is the power of the tongue. James 3:2 reveals that if you can control your tongue, you can control the rest of your body. This is referring to both your spoken words and your self-talk. A stronger statement in Proverbs 18:21 says, "the tongue has the power of life and death, and those who love it will eat its fruit." Power has been given to the tongues of people. Why? I speculate that it is because we are in the image of God, and when He spoke, He created everything out of nothing (Genesis 1:3).

When we speak, power is released. It is the power to build up and the power to tear down. This is the power of life and the power of death. It is the power of controlling even your own body. If you can control your tongue, you will see wonders happen. How important is this to God? Jesus states that every idle or careless word we speak will be judged (Matthew 12:36–37). Why? Because there is power in our tongues. So what are you confessing? Depression or life? You may want to consider being a "cup that is half full" type of person, because you are releasing something—either death or life.

It is your choice to utilize the spiritual laws presented here. I can say from experience that each one is very powerful when used in love toward God and toward people. You can change the world if you know that you are always sowing and reaping something, agreeing actively or inactively, and releasing life or death.

Read John chapter 19. Still yourself and place your-self in John 19:25–27. It is okay to come to Jesus and ask Him one of these questions:

> 1. How have I seen "sowing and reaping" in my life already?
>
> 2. What power do my words have?

Here is a place for you to write down any questions you have that came up while reading this lesson. Take your questions to a person of spiritual maturity that you trust.

Question: How can you begin using the spiritual laws?

# DAY 20:
NUMBER ONE!

What life is all about is really very simple: love. Someone came to Jesus one day and asked Him what was the greatest commandment. Jesus replied, "You shall love the Lord your God with all your heart, and with all your soul, and with all your mind. This is the great and foremost commandment. The second is like it, you shall love your neighbor as yourself" (Matthew 22:37–39). That's it. Love God, love yourself, and love people.

This is number one. If you miss this, you will miss the whole point of everything! Whatever you do, do not miss out of experiencing loving God, loving yourself, and loving people. Nothing else matters compared to this. If you do understand loving God, yourself, and others and believe it, you will have mastered the very meaning of life and found what millions are searching for.

Loving God seems pretty straightforward, but know that love is reciprocal. Many people do not have a problem giving love to God but have huge difficulty receiving love directed back to them. Love is not just given but received. If you want to fulfill the greatest commandment, you must give love to God and allow Him to love on you. It is wonderful to pray something like, "Papa God, I just want to sit on your lap." Using the soaking model of prayer can help you enter into a place where you can receive love from God. Loving Him could be singing to Him or obeying Him, which is the real backbone of worship (Romans 12:1).

Jesus said to love others as we love ourselves. Does God want you to love other people? Of course. First John 4:20 even goes so far as to say that we cannot truly love God without loving people. So yes, God wants us to love other people, but it has to flow from a heart that loves oneself. Receiving your identity in Christ is extremely important to being able to genuinely love others. Since I mentioned this on

Day 13, I will not belabor it. Only realize that God wants you to see yourself as He does…irresistible, royalty, and His dream come true!

Jesus gave us the best example of loving people. He knew who He was and loved people from that knowledge (John 13:3–5, "Jesus knowing that the father had given all things into His hands, and that He had come forth from God and was going to back to God, got up from supper, and laid aside His garments and taking a towel, He girded Himself. Then He poured water into the basin, and began to wash the disciples' feet and to wipe them with the towel with which He was girded"). Not only this, but He allowed people to love Him. Luke 7:37–38 records,

> "and there was a woman in the city who was a sinner; and when she learned that He was reclining at the table in the Pharisee's house, she brought an alabaster vial of perfume, and standing behind Him at His feet weeping, she began to wet His feet with her tears, and kept wiping them with the hair of her head, and kissing His feet and anointing them with the perfume."

That is why Jesus told us to love others the way He has loved us (John 13:34, "a new commandment I give to you, that you love one another, even as I have loved you, that you also love one another."). He was the perfect example of loving Himself and loving others.

Now listen to me carefully. You have a responsibility to the absolute number one commandment in the Bible. It is to love God and people. Some people call this "Christian Service." It is simply serving people as Jesus did. He came to serve (Mark 10:45). The love of God will compel you to serve other people. Know that God takes this commandment very seriously and is looking for you to walk in love (Matthew 25:31–46). A good chapter to read on love is *1* Corinthians 13. Walk in love, and you will fulfill all of the laws of God and live a fulfilling life (Matthew 22:40).

Read John chapter 20. Still yourself and place yourself in John 20:19–23. Receive the Holy Spirit and ask Jesus one of these questions:

1. How do I love those who are hard to love?
2. How much do you love me?

Here is a place for you to write down any questions you have that came up while reading this lesson. Take your questions to a person of spiritual maturity that you trust.

_____

_____

_____

Question: How does love handle being hurt by people even in church?

_____

_____

_____

DAY 21:
INCREASING

The purpose of this book is to help you understand some of your rights, privileges, and responsibilities as a follower of Jesus Christ. I showed some of the rights granted through the death and resurrection of Jesus, like being able to pray for the sick and see them healed. There were given privileges such as the chance at a genuine relationship with the most powerful and loving Being to ever exist. And I wrote about some responsibilities of being a member of the kingdom of heaven, like loving people and obeying God and His word (the Bible).

However, I would be doing you an injustice if I did not end this book with how you can go on from here. As you probably have seen by now, this book is a small snapshot of a supernatural life with God. There is much more to be learned in each subject and in many other subjects. This should not surprise you, considering how intelligent the God is that you serve. So I want to end this book with a story from Jesus that may help you know how to go from here.

Matthew 25:14–30 contains a powerful story called a *parable*. A parable is a type of story that Jesus uses which carries hidden meaning. In this parable, Jesus tells of someone that gives out a portion of money to three people. The money is called a *talent*, which was worth about fifteen years' wages of a laborer. One person received five talents, the second two talents, and the third one talent.

The person that gives the talents leaves for a certain amount of time then comes back to see what they have done with their talents. Both people who received the five talents and the two talents had doubled their money. However, the person that received the one talent buried his out of fear and gained nothing.

The parable ends terribly for the person with the one talent. His one talent is taken away and given to the person that increased to ten talents. If that was not bad enough, he was then thrown into eternal punishment, representing hell in the parable. Jesus ends the parable with these words: "Everyone who has, more shall be given, and he will have an abundance; but from the one who does not have, even what he does have shall be taken away."

Remember, this is a story with hidden meaning. This, as well as the other many parables that Jesus told, will give you deeper insight in the years to come. For this lesson, I want to focus on one thing Jesus said that I have not pointed out yet.

In verse 15, the parable states how the giver of the money chose how much money was given to each person. The decision was made according to each person's abilities. This is noteworthy because it will help you understand how God operates. Some people believe that God chooses everything for everyone and that we really have no say in the matter. While God does choose some people to do things, it is not the only way that God works. He looks at your abilities.

God gives abilities, and He also gives the ability to receive more abilities. By now you may be asking yourself, *What does this have to do with anything?* The point is this: you can gain more authority in God and more responsibility than right now by increasing your abilities. You will find that as you develop a closer relationship with God and increase your abilities, He will use you for greater things.

What I am teaching you here carries natural and supernatural implications. If you want to help with the worship team or in a small group meeting, then take instrument or voice lessons. Learn how to do web design or run a soundboard. Want to help with mission trips? Learn another language, and you will be surprised at the opportunities that open up to you. Learn to fix cars or fix up homes. Are you interested in art or dancing? Go for it! The very purpose of you being interested in something could be an invitation to pursue it.

I am not implying that increasing your abilities will be easy, but it will be worth it. Some people have been beaten down by the devil for so long that they do not know how to change. Those people may need to get a makeover. This may sound strange, but I promise that it can be life changing. Sometimes we have to change things in the natural to enable us to be set up for the supernatural. Increasing your abilities raises your potential to be a blessing to someone else.

Not only does this principle apply to the physical, but it also works in the spiritual. God increases what we already have when we do not bury it (or do not use it). Perhaps by now you are comfortable hearing God using two-way journaling. Add to this method hearing from God during the day. How? Ask Him what the next commercial on TV will be or the next song on the radio. Study prophecy, visions, and dreams. God rewards those who diligently seek Him. (Hebrews 11:6).

When you understand this truth, the Bible becomes an invitation instead of a study guide. Why? Because you have His promise that you can do the miracles He did (John 14:12). You have already been given that, and you have the ability to increase it. You increase anything in the spiritual realm by practicing it, being around those doing it, studying it, and asking God for it. Someone once said that more people are healed when you pray for more people.

Your invitation at the end of this book is to increase what you already have in God. As you increase in God, you will be given things that you did not even seek (Matthew 25:28). You can know God as much as you want. You can be used by God to do incredible things. Nothing is impossible for those that believe (Mark 9:23). What are you going to do with your faith?

Read John chapter 21. Still yourself and place yourself in John 21:12–14. Eat with Jesus and ask Him one of these questions:

> 1. What do I already have as talent(s) from you?
>
> 2. How can I increase in my abilities?

_____

_____

_____

_____

_____

_____

_____

Here is a place for you to write down any questions you have that came up while reading this lesson. Take your questions to a person of spiritual maturity that you trust.

_____

_____

_____

Question: What can you do today to increase your capacity?

_____

_____

_____

BOOKS OF THE BIBLE IN ORDER

Genesis	2 Chronicles	Daniel
Exodus	Ezra	Hosea
Leviticus	Nehemiah	Joel
Numbers	Esther	Amos
Deuteronomy	Job	Obadiah
Joshua	Psalms	Jonah
Judges	Proverbs	Micha
Ruth	Ecclesiastes	Nahum
1 Samuel	Song of Solomon	Habakkuk
2 Samuel	Isaiah	Zephaniah
1 Kings	Jeremiah	Haggai
2 Kings	Lamentations	Zechariah
1 Chronicles	Ezekiel	Malachi

Benjamin and Micah Joy Williams

Matthew	Ephesians	Hebrews
Mark	Philippians	James
Luke	Colossians	1 Peter
John	1 Thessalonians	2 Peter
Acts	2 Thessalonians	1 John
Romans	1 Timothy	2 John
1 Corinthians	2 Timothy	3 John
2 Corinthians	Titus	Jude
Galatians	Philemon	Revelation

You will have completely read the Gospel of John when you finish this book. After you have completed this book, I recommend reading the Bible over the course of one year.

This is an excellent way to get a good foundation. You can purchase a "One-Year Bible" at a local Christian bookstore or online. However, you may find a "read the Bible in a year plan" in the front or back of your Bible. If not, this can also be purchased online or at a local Christian bookstore.

CHRISTIAN LINGO

You may hear the following words or phrases in church or around Christians. These definitions are simple. For more thorough definitions refer to a Bible Dictionary like *The Eerdmans Bible Dictionary*. Edited by Allen C. Myers. *The Eerdmans Bible Dictionary* (Grand Rapids: Wm. B. Eerdmans Publishing Co., 1987)

Agape–a Greek word meaning God's type of love that is unselfish.

Amen–so be it. Used to end a prayer or agree with someone's prayer.

Apostle–Sent one. Can be a leader of leaders, church planter, and/or missionary. A leader in the Church (Ephesians 4:11).

Atonement–action done to cover sin by a priest in the Old Testament ultimately leading to Jesus dying on the cross to remove sin (Hebrews 10).

Backbiting–another word for gossip.

Bible Commentary–explains the Bible verse by verse.

Bible Dictionary–defines Bible terminology.

Blasted–see Slain the Spirit

Baptize–to immerse. Can refer to being water baptized (Day 18) or baptized in the Holy Spirit (Day 8).

Born Again–when someone gives their life to Christ.

Brother–a male fellow follower of Christ.

Christ–not the last name of Jesus. Actually means "Anointed One" or "Messiah" and refers to the one sent by God to save the world from being forever disconnected from God.

Christian–People who follow Christ.

Church - People who serve Jesus. Some refer to the building that the Church meets in as the church.

Demon–evil spirit beings. Most likely angels that turned against God.

Disciples–Twelve men Jesus called to personally follow Him; Simon called Peter, Andrew, James, John, Phillip, Bartholomew, Matthew, Thomas,

James the son of Alphaeus, Simon, Judas the son of James, and Judas Iscariot.

Evangelist–leader in church that is focused on leading people to Christ, revival, or training people in leading people to Christ.

Gospel (of the kingdom)–"good news" about God's kingdom coming here.

Gospels–The first four books in the New Testament; Matthew, Mark, Luke, and John

Grounded in the Word–deeply familiar with what the Bible says.

Hallelujah–praise God!

Harvest–new believers; reaping what is sown

Heaven–Eternal habitation of God, angels and followers of Christ.

Hell–Place designed for the devil and those that follow him.

In Jesus's Name–Accessing the provision of Christ (John 16:23).

Lost–A description of people before they become followers of Christ.

Messiah–Savior or liberator. Jesus is the Messiah of the world.

Pastor–someone leading a local church (Ephesians 4:11).

Pharisee - religious leaders in Jesus's day. Also see religious spirit.

Plead the Blood–claiming the provisions given through the death of Jesus.

Prophecy–recorded messages from God.

Prophesy–the act of telling someone a message from God.

Quiet Time–time set aside for prayer, reading the Bible, and listening to God.

Prophet–leader in the church (Ephesians 4:11). Someone God calls to give God's insight to the Church at large. It is different from prophesying.

Rapture–Greek word for being "caught up" (1 Thessalonians 4:16).

Religious Spirit–an attitude of pride in religious or moral actions (Matthew 23:27–28).

Revival–reviving what is dead. Could be special services at a church building where there is a supernatural increase of God's presence that leads to many people committing their lives to Christ and changes the community.

Sabbath–a day and a state of rest. (Exodus 20:8, Hebrews 4:1–11) The Old Testament has this as a day, namely Saturday. When Jesus was raised from the dead on Sunday much of the Church began calling Sunday the Sabbath (Matthew 28:1). Hebrews 4 speaks of the Sabbath rest as a position we have in God of being "at rest." In a relationship with God you no longer have to strive for a sense of rest. You merely need to receive this sense of rest and no longer be anxious again (Philippians 4:6).

Saint–someone forgiven by Christ and following Him.

Sanctified–set apart for God. Can do with holiness or being called by God to do something.

Saved–someone that has become a follower of Christ.

Shepherd–another word for pastor.

Sinner–someone that has broken the laws of God.

Sister–a female fellow follower of Christ.

Slain in the Spirit–where someone cannot stand up because of the power of the Holy Spirit on their body.

Stand in the gap–praying for other people (Ezekiel 22:30).

Strong's Concordance–book that lists out many words and where they can found in the Bible as well as the definitions in their original languages.

Teacher–leader in church (Ephesians 4:11). Someone that instructs people in the deep truths of the Bible.

Ten Commandments–rules given by God.

Tithe–a tenth of our earnings given to God through local church (Day 19).

Trinity–One God in expressing Himself as Father, Son (Jesus), and Holy Spirit (see Day 5).

Washed in the Blood–forgiven of sins.

Word–the Bible, prophecy, and Jesus.

NAMES OF GOD IN THE BIBLE

Credentials help us to gain an understanding of a per-son's abilities. Below is a list of Jesus' "credentials" that are listed in the Bible. These names will give you an idea of Jesus' abilities and of His heart. They are also good to use in prayer and worship. You can worship Jesus for who he is. For example you might pray, "Jesus I thank you for being Alpha and the Omega. You are the beginning and the end. You have been around for forever and I worship you for your greatness."

Advocate: 1 John 2:1

Amen: Revelation 3:14

Almighty: Revelation 1:8

Angel of the Lord: Genesis 16:7

Alpha: Revelation 1:8

Anointed One: Psalm 2:2

Apostle: Hebrews 3:1

Author and...

Beginning: Revelation 21:6

Bishop of Souls: 1 Peter 2:25

Branch: Zechariah 3:8

Bread of Life: John 6:35,48

Bridegroom: Matthew 9:15

Carpenter: Mark 6:3

Chief Shepherd: 1 Peter 5:4

The Christ: Matthew 1:16

Comforter: Jeremiah 8:18

Consolation of
Israel: Luke 2:25

Cornerstone: Ephesians 2:20

Dayspring: Luke 1:78

Day Star: 2 Peter 1:19

Deliverer: Romans 11:26

Desire of Nations: Haggai 2:7

Emmanuel: Matthew 1:23

End: Revelation 21:6

Everlasting Father: Isaiah 9:6

Faithful and True Witness:
Revelation 3:1

First Fruits:
1 Corinthians 15:23

Foundation: Isaiah 28:16

Fountain: Zechariah 13:1

Friend of Sinners:
Matthew 11:19

Horn of Salvation: Luke 1:69

Gate for the Sheep: John 10:7

I Am: Exodus: 3:14

Gift of God: 2
Corinthians 9:15

Jesus: Matthew 1:21

God: John 1:1

King of Israel Matthew 27:42

Glory of God: Isaiah 60:1

King of Kings:
Revelation 19:16

Good Shepherd: John 10:11

Lamb of God: John 1:29

Governor: Matthew 2:6

Last Adam:
1 Corinthians 15:45

Great Shepherd:
Hebrews 13:20

Life: John 14:6

Guide: Psalm 48:14

Light of the World: John 8:12

Head of the Church:
Colossians 1:18

Lion of the Tribe of Judah:
Rev. 5:5

High Priest: Hebrews 3:1

Lord or lords:
Revelation 19:16

Holy One of Israel:
Isaiah 41:4

Master: Matthew 23:8

Mediator: 1 Timothy 2:5

Messiah: John 1:41

Mighty God: Isaiah 9:6

Morning Star:
Revelation 22:16

Nazarene: Matthew 2:23

Omega: Revelation 1:8

Passover Lamb: 1
Corinthians 5:7

Perfecter of our Faith:
Hebrews 12:2

Physician: Matthew 9:12

Potentate: 1 Timothy 6:15

Priest: Hebrews 4:15

Prince of Peace: Isaiah 9:6

Prophet: Acts 3:22

Purifier: Malachi 3:3

Ransom: 1 Timothy 2:6

Redeemer: Isaiah 41:14

Refiner: Malachi 3:2

Refuge: Isaiah 25:4

Savior: Luke 1:47

Son of the Most
High: Luke 1:32

Teacher: Matthew 26:18

Word: John 1:1

And much more!

RECOMMENDED BOOKS OR MATERIALS

Day 1: Voice of God

James W. Goll and Michal Ann Goll, *Dream Language: The Prophetic Power of Dreams, Revelations, and the Spirit of Wisdom* (Shippensburg: Destiny Image, 2006)

Doug Addison, *Personal Development God's Way* (Shippensburg: Destiny Image, 2010), 179–200.

Mark Virkler and Pattie Virkler, *How to Hear God's Voice: An Interactive Learning Experience* (New York: Destiny Image, 2006).

Mark Virkler, *Hear God Through Your Dreams* (Buffalo: Virkler).

Joanthan Welton, *The School of the Seers* (Shippensburg: Destiny Imagine, 2009).

Bob Hazlett, *The Roar* (New Haven: Future Coaching Publications, 2013).

CD series. (www.touchoffire.org).

Day 2: The Kingdom

Rolland Baker and Heidi Baker, *Always Enough: God's Miraculous Provision among the Poorest Children on Earth* (New York: Baker Group, 2003).

Bill Johnson, *When Heaven Invades Earth* (Shippensburg: Destiny Image, 2005).

Don Williams, *Start Here: Kingdom Essentials for Christians* (New York: Regal Books, 2006).

Day 3: Belonging

Robert Coleman and Billy Graham, *The Master Plan of Evangelism* (Grand Rapids: Revell, 2006).

C. Peter Wagner, *Churchquake!* (New York: Regal Books, 1999).

Day 4: The Bible

Craig L. Blomberg, *The Historical Reliability of the Gospels* (New York: InterVarsity Press, 1987).

Gordon Fee and Douglas Stuart, *How To Read The Bible For All Its Worth: A guide to understanding the Bible* (Grand Rapids: Zondervan, 1990).

Mark Virkler, *Revelation Knowledge Versus Reasoned Knowledge and the Implications for Bible Colleges* (Communion With God Ministries) http:www.cwgministries.org/revelation-vs-reason.htm.

Jonathan Welton, *Understanding the Whole Bible* (Rochester: Jonathan Welton, 2014).

Day 5: The Cross

F.F. Bosworth, *Christ the Healer* (New York: Whitaker House, 2000).

John R. Stott and Alister McGrath, *The Cross of Christ* (New York: InterVarsity Press, 2006).

Contact New Life City Church at www.newlifecity.org about Pastor Alan Hawkin's audio message series, "The Emmaus Road."

Day 6: Faith

Stanley H. Frodsham, *Smith Wigglesworth: Apostle of Faith* (New York: Gospel House, 1990).

Kenneth E. Hagin, *Mountain-Moving Faith* (Tulsa: Faith Library Publications, Incorporated, 1993).

Kenneth Hagin, *The ABC's of Faith* (Recorded 2006). www.rhema.org

Joe McIntyre, *E.W. Kenyon and His Message of Faith: The True Story* (Lake Mary: Creation House, 1997).

Day 7: Prayer

Richard J. Foster, *Celebration of Discipline: The Path to Spiritual Growth* (London: Hodder & Stoughton Religious, 1998).

Dutch Sheets, *Intercessory Prayer: How God Can Use Your Prayers to Move Heaven and Earth* (Ventura: Regal Books, 2008).

Jeanne Guyon, *Experiencing the Depths of Jesus Christ* (Jacksonville: SeedSowers Christian Publishing, 1685).

Day 8: Spiritual Gifts

Randy Clark, *Baptism in the Holy Spirit* (Mechanicsburg: Global Awakening).

Donald Gee, *Concerning Spiritual Gifts* (Springfield: Gospel House, 1980).

Robby Dawkins, *Do What Jesus Did* (Bloomington: Chosen Books, 2013).

Day 9: Lend A Hand

Randy Clark, *There is More* (Mechanicsburg: Global Awakening, 2006).

Randy Clark, *School of Healing and Impartation: Revival Phenomena and Healing.* 5th ed. (Mechanicsburg: Global Awakening, 2008).

T.L. Osborn, *Healing the Sick: A Living Classic* (Tulsa: Harrison House)

Day 10: Witnessing

Doug Addison, *Prophecy, Dreams and Evangelism: Revealing Through Diving Encounters* (New Hampshire: Streams Publishing House, 2005).

Che' Ahn, *Fire Evangelism: Reaching the Lost thought Love and Power* (Grand Rapids: Chosen Books, 2006).

Reinhard Bonnke, *Evangelism by Fire: Igniting Your Passion for the Lord* (London: Full Flame GmbH, 2002).

Randy Clark, *Power, Holiness, Evangelism: Rediscovering God's Purity, Power and Passion for the Lost* (Shippensburg: Destiny Image, 1999).

Jerry Cooke, *Love, Acceptance and Forgiveness* (Ventura: Regal Books, 1979).

Mark Driscoll, *The Radical Reformission: Reaching Out without Selling Out* (Grand Rapids: Zondervan, 2004).

T. L. Osborn, *Soulwinning* (Tulsa: Harrison House, 1980).

Rebecca Pippert, *Out of the Saltshaker and into the World: Evangelism as a way of Life* (Downers Grove: InterVarsity Press, 1999).

Day 11: Who You Are

John Eledredge and Stasi Eldredge, *Captivating: Unveiling the Mystery of a Woman's Soul* (Danbury: Thomas Nelson, Inc., 2005).

John Eldredge, *Wild at Heart: Discovering the Secret of a Man's Soul* (Danbury: Thomas Nelson Inc., 2003).

Kenneth Hagin E., *The Believer's Authority* (Tulsa: Rhema, 1984).

Leif Hetland, *Healing the Orphan Spirit, revised additional* (Peachtree City: Global Awareness, 2011).

Trisha Frost, *Unbound* (Shippensburg: Destiny Image, 2012).

Day 12: History

Thomas Bokenkotter, *A Concise History of the Catholic*

Church (Garden City: Image, 2005).

Eddie L. Hyatt, *2000 Years of Charismatic Christianity: A 21st Century Look at Church History* (Lake Mary: Charisma House, 2002).

Roberts Liardon, *God's Generals I: Why They Succeeded and Why Some Failed* (New Kensington: Whitaker House, 2003).

Elmer L. Towns, Douglas Porter, and Elmer Towns, *The Ten Greatest Revivals Ever* (Ann Harbor: Servant Publications, 2000).

J. Edward Morris, Cindy McCowan, and Tom Welchel, *They Told Me Their Stories: The Youth and Children of Azusa Street Tell Their Stories* (Mustang, Dare2Dream, 2006)

Philip Jenkins, *The Lost History of Christianity: The Thousand Year Golden Age* (New York: HarperOne, 2008).

Day 13: The Heart

Jack Frost, *Experiencing Father's Embrace* (Shippensburg: Destiny Image, 2006).

Rodney Hogue, *Forgiveness* (Hayward, CA: Rodney Hogue, 2006).

John Sandford, Paula Sandfard, Loren Sandford, *Transforming the Inner Man: God's Powerful Principles for Inner Healing and Lasting Life Change* (Lake Mary: Charisma House, 2007).
Micah Williams, *Christ the Wonderful Counselor* ebook (www.releasinglife.com)

Day 14: Repentance

Charles G. Finney, *True and False Repentance* (Minneapolis: Kregel Publications, 1981).

Bill Johnson, *Supernatural Power of the Transformed Mind* (Shippensburg: Destiny Image, 2005).

Day 15: Holiness

Randy Clark, *Power, Holiness, Evangelism: Rediscovering God's Purity, Power and Passion for the Lost* (Shippensburg: Destiny Image, 1999).

Sergio Scataglini, *The Fire of His Holiness: Preparing Yourself to Enter God's Presence* (Springfield: Gospel Light, 1999).

Day 16: Judgment

John Bunyan, *The Resurrection of the Dead and Eternal Judgment* (Glasgow: Blackie & Son, 1873).

Day 17: Jesus' Return

Jonathan Welton, *Raptureless third addition* (Rochester: Jonathan Welton, 2015).

Harold Eberle and Martin Trench, *Victorious Eschatology : A Partial Preterist View* (GrandRapids: Worldcast, 2007 Second Edition).

Day 18: Sacraments

Perry Stone, *The Meal That Heals : Enjoying Intimate, Daily Communion with God* (Lake Mary: Charisma House, 2008).

Day 19: Spiritual Law

Charles G. Finney, *Charles G. Finney's Systematic Theology : The Complete and Newly Expanded 1878 Edition from One of America's Greatest Evangelists* (Ada: Bethany House, 1994).

Day 20: Number One!

Rolland Baker and Heidi Baker, *Always Enough : God's Miraculous Provision among the Poorest Children on Earth* (Ada: Baker Group, 2003).

Jerry Cooke, *Love, Acceptance and Forgiveness* (Ventura: Regal Books, 1979).

Day 21: Increase

Bill Johnson, *Dreaming with God : Secrets to Redesigning Your World Through God's Creative Flow,* (Shippensburg: Destiny Image, 2006).

Steve Hickey, *Obtainable Destiny* (Boston: Strang Communications Company, 2004).

Doug Addison, *Personal Development God's Way* (Shippensburg: Destiny Image, 2010).

Ron McIntosh, *The Greatest Secret: God's Law of Attraction for Lasting Happiness, Fulfillment, Health and Abundance in Life* (Lakeland: White Stone Books, 2007).

Rolland Baker and Heidi Baker, *There is Always Enough: God's Miraculous Provision among the Poorest Children on Earth* (Grand Rapids: Chosen Books, 2002).

Leif Hetland, *Giant Slayer* (Shippensburg: Destiny Image, 2017).

MORE RECOMMENDED BOOKS

John Crowder, *Miracle Workers, Reformers, and the New Mystics : How to Become Part of the Supernatural Generation* (Shippensburg: Destiny Image, 2006).

Jim Cymbala and Dean Merrill. *Fresh Wind, Fresh Fire: What Happens When God's Spirit Invades the Hearts of His People* (Grand Rapids: Zondervan, 2003).

Ted Dekker and Bill Bright, *Blessed Child* (Danbury: Thomas Nelson Incorporated, 2001).

Mark Driscoll and Gerry Breshears, *Death by Love* (Wheaton: Crossway Books, 2008).

Mark Driscoll and Gerry Breshears, *Vintage Jesus : Timeless Answers to Timely Question* (Wheaton: Crossway Books, 2008).

Gene Edwards, *A Tale of Three Kings : A Study of Brokenness* (Carol Stream: Tyndale House, 1995).

Becky Fischer, *Redefining Children's Ministry in the 21ˢᵗ Century* (Mandan: Kids in Ministry International, 2005).

Lee Grady, *Ten Lies the Church Tells Women : How the Bible Has Been Misused to Keep Women in Spiritual Bondage* (Lake Mary: Charisma House, 2000).

Benny Hinn, *Good Morning, Holy Spirit* (Nashville: Thomas Nelson Publishers, 1997).

Rick Joyner, *The Final Quest* (Fort Mill: MorningStar Publications, Incorporated, 2006).

Matt Redman, *The Unquenchable Worshipper : Coming Back to the Heart of Worship* (Ventura: Regal Books, 2004).

Arthur Wallis, *God's Chosen Fast* (Danbury: Christian Literature Crusade, Incorporated, 1993).

SPECIAL THANKS

I would like to thank Randy Clark for taking the time to read the book of a "little ol' me." You are truly a gift to the Body of Christ and an inspira-tion to me. It has been easy to see your love for peo-ple and for God while attending Global School of Supernatural Ministry. Thank you for imparting the heart of God to us!

Thank you to Ryan Adair, Dr. David Nichols of Heart of the Father Ministries, and M. Caleb Mabry for your input on the recommended books. Your insight will help people dive deeper into the things of God.

Thank you to all the people and especially Joseph Cotten that read through the book and helped me with editing, input and encouragement.

Thank you also to Dale Mast of http://www. dalemast.com/ for his prophetic encouragement to write this book. I also want to thank Bob Hazlett of http://www.touchoffire.org/ for his prophetic encouragement.

Phill Olson, you were kind enough to read this book and assist in shaping it so that it could be used as an effective tool. With your help in getting this book out, I hope many people are touched. Thank you for all your selfless work and well-timed hugs. May the Lord continue to use you to "Phill (fill) others." Thank you also to Curt Maloy for helping in the editing process.

I also send a special thank you to Pastor Murphy Matheny for sparking the fire of discipleship in my heart many years ago. A special thanks also to Pastors Mike Smith, Max Myers, and Steven Abbott for fueling the flame of discipleship each in your own way. May the churches be filled with disciples!

This book would be completely unnecessary without the love of Jesus being spread through his witnesses. I send out a huge thank you to anyone who is reaching out to the lost and hurting!

I especially want to thank the most beautiful woman in the world, my wife. Micah Joy, you are my best, and I love you. Thank you for putting up with my passion to write this book. You spent so much time editing and making suggestions on this book that it is easily said that we wrote this together. Thank you for believing in me and not being afraid to tell me when you thought something was written poorly. Without you, this book would not exist. Thank you, Babe!

Finally, I want to thank my first love, God. You are so amazing and patient with me. Thank you for laying out a beautiful and mysterious plan.

ABOUT THE AUTHORS

Benjamin is an ordained minister through ANGA, www.globalawakening.com. He has earned a bachelor's degree in evangelism from North Central University Minneapolis, Minnesota as well as completed a total of four additional years of ministry school training through Master's Commission and Global School of Supernatural Ministry. Benjamin has had the privilege of working for Billy Graham Association, A/G MN District Council, Global Awakening, and InLight Connection. He has traveled full time and been an Outreach and Discipleship Pastor. Benjamin is the founder and president of Life Ministries International. He has been traveling and preaching since he was sixteen and has led over 3,000 people to become followers of Jesus Christ. His passion is to raise up selfless Christ-lovers who know their identity, authority, and responsibility to influence culture with the kingdom of heaven.

Micah has a similar passion and story as Ben. She is a licensed minister through ANGA, www.globala-wakening.com, earned a bachelor's degree in church music from North Central University, Minneapolis, Minnesota and has had the privilege to work for Global Awakening and InLight Connection. Micah has been a Creative Arts Pastor, Director of Worship, and has played on worship teams with Steve Swanson, Julie Meyer, and JoAnn MacFatter. Her passion is for prayer ministry and the presence of the Lord. Micah has facilitated training from Elijah House and has led or helped with worship in a variety of settings from a few people to several thousand.

Benjamin and Micah live in Harrisburg, PA, with their incredible daughter, Zoé Joy Delight Williams.

Life Ministries International is available for ministry. They are often called on to minister from the passions they have. Commitments to follow Christ, healings, and encouraging words from God are common in their meetings. Benjamin is also available to be an "evangelist consultant" to local churches wanting to feed a revival culture. If you would like to have them minister in an event or help you with discipleship consultation, email lmi.contact@gmail.com. For more information go to www.basics21.com.

Made in the USA
Las Vegas, NV
15 December 2021

37881645R00101